SHIFT

A New Mindset for Sustainable Execution

SHIFT

A New Mindset for
Sustainable Execution

M. KATHRYN BROHMAN, PHD,
EILEEN BROWN, AND
JIM MCSHEFFREY

UNIVERSITY OF TORONTO PRESS
Toronto Buffalo London

ISBN 978-1-4875-0378-9

This book is made of recycled materials
and other controlled sources.

Library and Archives Canada Cataloguing in Publication

Title: Shift : a new mindset for sustainable execution /
M. Kathryn Brohman, Eileen Brown, and Jim McSheffrey.

Names: Brohman, M. Kathryn, author. |
Brown, Eileen, author. | McSheffrey, Jim, author.

Description: Includes bibliographical references and index.

Identifiers: Canadiana 20190149310 | ISBN 9781487503789 (hardcover)

Subjects: LCSH: Organizational effectiveness. |
LCSH: Strategic planning. | LCSH: Organizational change.

Classification: LCC HD58.9 .B76 2019 | DDC 658.4/013 – dc23

University of Toronto Press acknowledges the financial assistance to its
publishing program of the Canada Council for the Arts and the Ontario
Arts Council, an agency of the Government of Ontario.

Canada Council   Conseil des Arts
for the Arts   du Canada

ONTARIO ARTS COUNCIL
CONSEIL DES ARTS DE L'ONTARIO
an Ontario government agency
un organisme du gouvernement de l'Ontario

Funded by the   Financé par le
Government   gouvernement
of Canada   du Canada

Canadä

MIX
Paper from
responsible sources
FSC® C103567

CONTENTS

ABOUT THE AUTHORS

Professor Kathryn Brohman, PhD, an academic scholar with over twenty years' experience as a researcher, consultant, and executive educator in technology, project management, and Agile management methods, was joined by two accomplished executives, each with over thirty-five years of experience and reputations for their ability to execute. The team's collective expertise came from time spent in highly integrated business environments such as supply chain, enterprise systems, mergers and acquisitions, and human capital management to validate the concepts and transform ideas into practical application. Eileen Brown started her career with IBM Canada and was part of the Mergers & Acquisition team that built the global footprint of Celestica, a spinoff company. She has held global vice president roles in Supply Chain, IT, and HR in high-tech companies such as Celestica and BlackBerry. Jim McSheffrey spent his career at 3M and held senior executive roles, including president and general manager of 3M Canada, and managing director of both 3M UK and 3M China. Together the team of three formulated the conceptual frameworks and inspired best practices to support Dr Brohman's underlying research.

PREFACE

Organizations create impressive strategies but fail too often in their attempts to get results. Despite advances in leadership and new approaches to managing change, ongoing research claims 80 per cent of leaders feel their company is good at crafting strategy but only 44 per cent are confident in their ability to implement it.[1] Several notable books have been published on the subject of execution, yet organizations continue to struggle. So what is missing or getting in the way? One school of thought is that driving results in today's turbulent environment requires that business practices be both flexible and stable. However, too much flexibility can exhaust resources and too much stability can lead to barriers such as "Sorry, the system won't let me do that," leaving customers disappointed.[2]

This book explains how companies can balance flexibility and stability by removing "drag" – a competing force to execution that obstructs the delivery of results and causes valuable organizational energy to be misdirected and wasted. It was the importance of managing energy[3] that evolved from our work with over 750 organizations and inspired the concept of *sustainable execution*. Using a wind turbine analogy, readers are taken on a journey where barriers causing drag are defined and best practices for removing barriers are explored. The result is an improved capability for driving short-term results without compromising long-term success.

So how do organizations get started on a path to sustainable execution? The first step is to categorize execution challenges into *twelve barriers* to diagnose the causes of execution failure and understand the *three execution levers* (structure, rhythm, and awareness) that need to be orchestrated to resolve them. Using our propriety measure called the Cost of Execution (CO_x), organizations can quantify drag and use this performance indicator to determine the need for improvements in their execution system. The second step identifies specific ways that organizations can improve their execution system. Our *Shift-to-Execute* framework prescribes four actions that we call "shifts," which stabilize a backbone for execution by *filling gaps before removing distractions* to accelerate work as well as adjust and readjust to changes in the environment. To understand why this step is important, think about the last time you have had to "work around" a policy or procedure to get something done. This is a result of too much stability. Now recall the last time a quality problem escaped your internal controls resulting in a customer complaint. This was likely caused by trying to do too much or go too fast. Working through the book's chapters, readers will learn how real organizations achieve both flexibility and stability by filling gaps and removing distractions.

Written to provide a pragmatic approach to making improvements, the book is structured into four parts so readers can navigate through the chapters in a way that best suits their needs.

- **Part One: Identifying Execution Barriers.** Explains the fundamental framework and concepts that differentiate sustainable execution from other execution models. We identify and categorize twelve execution barriers and the three execution levers that resolve them – *structure, rhythm,* and *awareness,* the latter being novel compared to other execution models. Part one also associates sustainable execution to managing execution as a "system of energy" to drive short-term results without compromising long-term success.

- **Part Two: Filling the Gaps.** Chapters in this section explain how organizations *shift* to fill gaps in their backbone to stabilize the execution system. In the energy analogy, the backbone builds new *sources of energy* by unleashing the capacity to do more with less and generating momentum.

- **Part Three: Removing Distractions.** Chapters in this section explain how organizations *shift* to remove distractions and enhance flexibility. The energy analogy highlights the importance of efficient *energy consumption* by promoting collaboration and focusing on what is most important.

- **Part Four: The Sustainable Execution Leader.** This final part of the book explains one additional source of drag that is not addressed by filling gaps and removing distractions – poor leadership. This section defines the traits that differentiate execution leaders from other leaders in the organization. Wrapping up the book this way, we provide readers with the opportunity to reflect on how they drive results, not only in their job, but in other aspects of their life.

SHIFT

A New Mindset for Sustainable Execution

PART ONE

Identifying Execution Barriers

Using our research, the next two chapters define the twelve most common execution barriers and introduce the idea of orchestrating balance between three execution levers (structure, rhythm, and awareness) to improve an organization's ability to consistently deliver results. Readers are also provided with a new measurement or key performance indicator (KPI) that can be used to identify barriers and monitor improvements to their execution system. The Cost of Execution (CO_x) factor is proprietary to our research and is a valuable tool in achieving a state of sustainable execution.

Finally, part one introduces our Shift-to-Execute framework that conceptualizes a pathway to improving sustainability and lowering the overall cost of execution. A unique aspect of the framework is the differentiation between gaps and distractions in the execution system. Missing pieces (gaps) need to be addressed before diving deeper, to uncover things that are getting in the way (distractions).

Sustainable Execution Diagnostic Assessment (SEDA)

Part one makes reference to an online supplement to the book called SEDA (available at www.sustainableexecution.ca). SEDA is an assessment tool that conducts a rigorous analysis of execution barriers.

Results assist organizations in identifying their top barriers, determining a score for each execution lever (structure, rhythm, awareness), and calculating their CO_x factor and sustainability. Hundreds of organizations have used this tool to generate a range of benefits described in chapter 1.

1

A NEW MINDSET FOR EXECUTION

Why do some organizations drive results year after year while their competitors seem to come and go? Why are some sport franchises always at or near the top of their league, despite continuous changes to their roster and management team? Why can individuals with a résumé almost identical to their predecessor's drive significantly better results? In the past, differences would be attributed to leadership, strategy, and the ability to manage change. More recently however, attention has been given to the subject of "execution" – the ability to realize the best possible results on what you have set out to do. Organizations that traditionally invested heavily in developing their strategy understand that great strategy is worthless if they can't execute it. Execution encourages organizational leaders to acknowledge strategy and execution as two sides of the same coin and question why investments in the latter have lagged. In fact, in many cases, execution has been delegated "down" the organization, and in hindsight the inability to deliver results should have been predictable.

Most organizations define poor execution as the inability to deliver anticipated financial results consistently, quarter after quarter. Other common execution failures include delivering a project late or over budget, pulling the plug on a technology investment, or failing to retain your most valued customers. However, this book addresses the reality that the day-to-day whirlwind of activity behind achieving short-term results is not always productive. Poor communication, competing priorities, and overbearing compliance can be problematic, even when organizations display conventional signs of executing well. Below are some real-world examples:

- A financial organization that delivered quarterly results by setting unrealistic goals that pushed employees to a state of fatigue and exhaustion;
- A project in commercial real estate that delivered on time but incurred additional risk by squeezing the schedule at the expense of quality and compliance;
- A new information system, implemented at a health services organization, that people were forced to use to capture data at a cost of reduced efficiency and increased frustration; and
- A high-end retailer so focused on customer retention that they failed to invest in new business opportunities and, as a result, were driven to the point of bankruptcy.

Setting unrealistic goals, squeezing the schedule, mandating behavior, and establishing competing objectives are all examples of "barriers" that impede sustainable execution. Essential to our perspective is the idea that execution barriers impede performance, as they reduce the *executional energy* of the organization. Contrary to barriers are more recognized execution enablers such as setting clear goals, doing work in stages, celebrating milestones, establishing accountability, and providing feedback. After examining execution in over 750 organizations, we've learned why these enablers help to fill gaps in the organization's backbone, but this is only half the story. The other half is a commitment to removing distractions inherent in today's business environment (e.g., increased speed of doing business, complex regulation, information overload, etc.). This book encourages organizations to adopt a new mindset for execution that starts with identifying barriers that build up and cause execution to break down. Many barriers, specifically those causing distraction, can be difficult to detect because their impact it not linked to outright failure. They cause a slow deterioration of performance over time. As such, using an *organization as a system of energy* analogy, we define the impact of execution barriers as sources of friction or drag that holds back progress and wears down resources. When organizations allow barriers to go unnoticed, drag on execution energy increases and conventional failures begin to emerge.

To illustrate, let's examine Boutique Financial,[1] a small financial services firm that experienced a shortfall three years into executing an ambitious five-year growth strategy. Using the sustainable execution lens, our team found evidence of execution barriers causing drag that dated all the way back to Year 1. Specifically, performance targets established as part of the growth strategy were so aggressive that directors, who were not included in the strategy discussions, were not convinced they were achievable. Directors tried to express their concern multiple times, but the executive team was steadfast – the strategy was set and directors needed to execute it. In an effort to address their concern, leadership introduced new director-level incentives to reward results. Boutique Financial met financial targets in Year 1.

In Year 2, despite incentives, the organization's culture started to break down. Casual water cooler conversations decreased to a minimum and the new incentive structure actually made departments more protective of their resources and less willing to work together. Although employees were becoming more and more disengaged, somehow Boutique Financial managed to deliver on the financial targets once again.

Description of Sustainable Execution Research

Our research study launched in 2012 by conducting fifty-seven semi-structured interviews with executives and managers in 17 organizations to identify the preliminary list of execution barriers. From 2013 to 2015, open-ended surveys were completed by managers and executives across 245 organizations, and analysis converged on twelve execution barriers. Building on previous academic research in organizational energy and organizational agility, survey data were analyzed to quantify drag and identify three execution levers (structure, rhythm, and awareness) that enable organizations to achieve both short-term and long-term results. In 2016, the Sustainable Execution Diagnostic Assessment (SEDA) was developed and launched; 362 Cost of Execution (CO_x) assessments were completed, and the impact on performance was assessed. Results were also used to determine the coefficients used in the SEDA online tool. Finally, from 2016 to 2018, 168 organizations participated in a study that described how their organizations removed barriers to improve. It was analysis from this study, specifically the difference between filling gaps and removing distractions, that the Shift-to-Execute framework emerged.

See H. Bruch and S. Ghosha, "Unleashing Organizational Energy: Four Types of Organizational Energy Can Either Stimulate or Handicap Competitiveness," *MIT Sloan Management Review* 45, no. 1 (2003): 45–52; C.G. Worley and E.E. Lawler, "Agility and Organization Design: A Diagnostic Framework," *Organizational Dynamics* 39, no. 2 (2010): 194–204.

By Year 3, five directors resigned and the organization had become saturated with blame, excuses, and lack of trust. The drag on performance had become too significant and execution barriers finally took their toll. The once highly collaborative, autonomous, focused organization no longer had the energy required to overcome the drag from mounting execution barriers. On the heels of failure, leadership set out to find a pathway for improvement.

Pathway for Improvement

The Year 3 shortfall was especially problematic for Boutique Financial, as funding for the five-year growth strategy was provided by an equity party who contracted a claw-back penalty (50 per cent of the shortfall) to be paid if performance targets were not met. Desperate to prevent another penalty payment, Boutique Financial was eager to make improvements. Our team encouraged them to start by reallocating resources to focus on what was most important – growth. Boutique Financial had been operating with lean management principles[2] for years. However, the new strategy had adjusted priorities. The focus on growth resulted in sales representatives being asked to do too much and other areas of the business left operating with excess capacity. To improve, work was redesigned in Year 4 and a new Sales support team was formed. Directors also agreed to share director-level incentives with Sales and Support in an effort to motivate performance.

Next, Boutique Financial realized the lean initiative had optimized business processes in a way that transformed work to focus more on process than results. Although the disciplined, systematic approach increased efficiency, it reduced the latitude and autonomy people needed to create new ways to increase growth. Process had stifled the regular, open communication and feedback that once filled the halls at Boutique Financial and helped keep people aligned and productive. To improve, leadership at Boutique Financial agreed to reduce the number of performance metrics being used to monitor process performance (e.g., number of sales leads, number of investor plans completed) and focus more on metrics that measured results (e.g., new sales dollars). They also assigned an owner to each business process who had the authority to alter work activities as required. Coaching leadership at Boutique Financial was a great experience because they were eager to learn and highly committed to filling their execution gaps. However, when the company experienced their second shortfall at the end of Year 4, some leadership became skeptical and questioned whether these changes had actually put them on the right path for improvement.

Key to our engagement with Boutique Financial in Year 5 was convincing leadership to change their mindset for execution by realizing no single, silver bullet or best practice could guarantee the prevention of another shortfall. We agreed that the new Sales support team, adjusted performance metrics, and process owners filled some crucial *gaps* in their execution backbone. However, the Year 4 shortfall was evidence that *distractions* were still getting in their way. We drew their attention to the five directors who left the organization in Year 3 and had an open and honest conversation about why they left. Leadership had their own opinions, and all agreed their departure contributed to the shortfall but admitted they had not invested a lot of time and energy to fully understand what caused them to leave. Opening up an inquiry that involved talking to employees, executives realized the incentive structure they implemented had some unforeseen negative consequences. Specifically, departments had become extremely protective of their resources and started competing with one another. Leadership responded by

relocating a few employees across departments to inspire collaboration in hopes the change would improve culture through relationship building and trust. In addition, they came up with the idea to
implement a "sale-a-thon,"[3] where employees come together for an
entire day each quarter to brainstorm new ideas and strategies for
growth. The impact on culture was almost immediate, as Boutique
Financial had always been a highly collaborative organization, so
returning to their roots was a natural and welcomed transition.

Most significant to Boutique Financial's pathway to improvement was a change inspired at a meeting where leadership were
encouraged to revisit the feasibility of performance targets dating
back to Year 1. As expected, this suggestion met with resistance; one
C-suite executive in particular strongly articulated his frustration
and annoyance. Through reflection and discussion, leadership recognized their optimism and expectation for growth had interfered
with their willingness to listen to the directors' concerns. They agreed
to revisit the targets, and this time around they would include the
directors in the discussions. This decision piqued frustration for the
one C-suite executive; weeks after this meeting he resigned from
the company. In collaboration with directors, adjustments to Year 5
targets were made and projections extended for an additional
three years. They presented the new strategy to the equity partner,
who had been kept apprised of Boutique Financial's pathway for
improvement. They agreed to help finance the three-year extension
on one condition – Boutique Financial had to meet their adjusted
targets for Year 5. They did.

Wrapping up the Boutique Financial engagement, leadership realized that if they had listened to their directors in the beginning, short-
falls could have likely been prevented. Their mindset for execution
was no longer limited to conventional signs of executing well. Even
when times were good, they implemented a continuous regimen of
identifying execution barriers early and making improvements.

New Mindset: Orchestrating the Balancing Act

This book contributes to a series of others intending to modernize execution practices. In 2002, Larry Bossidy, Ram Charan, and Charles Burck brought execution to the forefront and inspired organizations to develop systematic processes for getting things done.[4] They tasked leadership with the responsibility of hiring the right people, making tough decisions, and taking accountability for delivering results. Sustainable execution contributes to modern execution practice by simplifying execution into three execution levers and using those levers to orchestrate the *balancing act*.

- **Structural Levers:** For decades organizations have executed their strategy by shaping structure (e.g., roles, authority, rewards, metrics, plans, tools, talent, etc.) to align to the most important goals and objectives.[5] In sustainable execution, structural levers allocate resources and drive alignment by formalizing roles and reporting relationships, and establishing appropriate controls and incentive systems to motivate and guide behavior.
- **Rhythm Levers:** Modern execution thinking highlights the importance of *rhythm* to accelerate execution and help organizations be more proactive and pivot seamlessly when the need arises.[6] In sustainable execution, rhythm levers ensure the execution system is responsive and productive, day in and day out, by establishing processes, accountability, and a sense of urgency while promoting consistency and predictability at the same time. It is rhythm that keeps people focused on the right priorities and fosters agility.
- **Awareness Levers:** Maintaining a state of awareness is novel to sustainable execution. It is an organization's ability to fill gaps and mitigate distractions to improve the sensing and exploitation of new opportunities. Awareness levers foster the creation of

a culture for execution that pays attention to what is really going on and takes appropriate action. When a culture for execution is achieved, organizations promote objective decision-making, break down silo mentality, and remove bias and blinders to enhance the organization's ability to get things done.

Conceptually, *orchestrating the balancing act* is an execution practice that keeps structure, rhythm, and awareness in state of balance. Balance does not mean that the three execution levers are employed equally; it means organizations need to alter the relative frequency with which each lever is used, to fine-tune performance. To provide a practical example, let's return to Boutique Financial. Their pathway to improvement began by reallocating resources and creating the new Sales support team – we call that "turning up structure." This change was complemented by a "turn up in rhythm," as the new approach encouraged autonomy and open communication. Finally, in Year 5 the organization "turned up awareness" to inquire why the five directors left and address the inherent leadership issues amongst the C-suite executives.

As the Boutique Financial example illustrates, the balancing act transforms execution leadership into the likes of an *orchestra conductor* who knows when to tone down trumpets so flutes can make their impact. Identifying barriers is only the first step; orchestration highlights the need to take subsequent action. In fact, noticing barriers but failing to take subsequent action is the most common cause of execution failure. Failure is also caused by investing in one improvement without considering its impact on other execution factors. Take, for example, an organization that "turns up" awareness to promote employee engagement as a way to motivate performance but does not "turn down" structure, so excessive control continues to unnecessarily burden day-to-day work. The result is counterproductive. As such, orchestrating balance acts as an *equalizer* in the

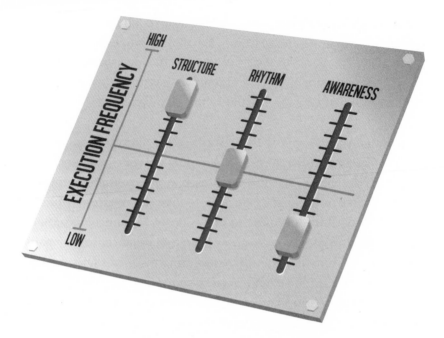

Figure 1.1 Orchestrating the Balancing Act

organization's execution system (figure 1.1). Organizations alter the relative frequencies of structure, rhythm, and awareness to not only enhance performance, but more importantly, filter out distractions and barriers that are getting in the way.

Orchestrating balance encourages organizations to abandon the underlying *choisir une voie* mentality that suggests execution practice needs to "pick a lane" between practices that drive results through stability and those that promote flexibility. Management control and process create discipline, and knowing who reports to whom establishes clear lines of authority and accountability. Low-rule environments are deemed more agile, and distributing decision rights promises to make organizations more flexible. Because the rules of hierarchy collide with the ground rules of practices that promote agility, organizations mistakenly assume that stability and flexibility cannot work together effectively. In sustainable execution, even if organizations have an underlying preference, the ability to orchestrate structure, rhythm, and awareness to work together is imperative to executing well. For example, "turning up" awareness can help highly structured organizations realize the need to "turn down" structure to alleviate outdated policies and/or controls that create undue burdens on day-to-day work. "Turning up" rhythm can be as simple as helping coordinate people across diverse geographies by opening up lines of communication and establishing clear priorities. Finally, "turning up" structure to heighten objectivity can help people communicate better at a time when key decisions are being made that affect the entire organization. Our work in helping organizations orchestrate the balancing act has uncovered a few fundamental rules that describe a new mindset for sustainable execution:

1 Orchestration does not favor one lever over another – even if an organization or leader has a preference for one of the three levers, all are needed to enhance performance and filter out barriers.
2 Balance cannot be established once or twice a year – orchestration is a continuous practice of oversight and feedback. Accurate assessment of the current situation, making improvements, and reassessing balance is necessary to addressing barriers that emerge.
3 Getting balance "right" is fleeting – the first quarter in which an organization rests on its past success and stops listening to what's going on around it is likely the same moment execution starts to break down.
4 The balancing act needs to be prioritized as an important management initiative. When execution barriers are repeatedly ignored, the system of execution will break down.

5 Finally, if execution is not working in your organization, doing what you've always done faster and with fewer resources will not enable the changes you need to improve.

What Is Sustainable Execution?

A PwC study published in 2012 stated only 40 per cent of organizations declared they were successful at executing on their strategy, down from 90 per cent thirty years ago.[7] So something in the execution landscape has changed. Rapidly evolving business models driven by technological change, political turbulence, mounting regulatory pressures, and social and environmental demands put immense pressure on organizations to execute above and beyond achieving short-term, bottom-line results. As such, the premise of sustainable execution is simple: *it requires the identification of execution barriers so organizations can optimize energy needed to deliver short-term results without losing sight of long-term goals.* According to McKinsey & Company, 70 per cent of organizations fail or fall significantly short of fulfilling their initiatives for improvement and change.[8] Some make significant progress in the short term, only to see those positive changes fade away. When organizations execute in sustainable ways, they achieve the following results:

- They are able to *respond to market forces* more rapidly by preventing energy from being spent unproductively, *continuously improving and having the ability to make change "stick."* Execution makes progress toward improvement goals, and change initiatives are effectively infused into the day-to-day whirlwind of activity.
- They are capable of *bouncing back and recovering from difficulty.* In 2017 the International Organization for Standardization (ISO) introduced ISO 22316 – a framework for organizations to

future-proof their business through security and resilience. Climate change, economic crisis, and security vulnerabilities are just some of the pitfalls that require organizations to be more resilient by absorbing and adapting to unpredictability while continuing to deliver on the goals and objectives to drive results.

- They *do not lose sight of long-term viability for short-term gain*. It is common for immediate demands to take precedence over longer-term goals and objectives; however, driving short-term results should not come at a significant cost to the ongoing viability of the business. Driving results should not excuse employee burn-out or unethical behavior.

- They *sustain profit and customers*. More and more, companies are engaging in online, direct-to-customer strategies to achieve greater profits, making customer loyalty more difficult to achieve. In many ways, execution is the only strategy customers see, so sustainable organizations must learn how to attract and reattract their customers. Today's customers are more discerning and have greater expectations; they expect companies to anticipate and keep pace with their changing demands.

Building on our system of energy analogy, the competing force to sustainable execution is drag. Execution barriers reduce sources of energy that build capacity and generate momentum, interfere with conservative use of energy by impeding synergy, and ineffectively ground energy needed to focus work and prevent leaks. Organizations will naturally find ways to compensate for drag over a short period of time; however, executing in this way is not sustainable. Boutique Financial is a real example of this. They learned the hard way that energy will eventually deplete if execution barriers are not addressed. Employee engagement is a common example of energy that when managed well can enhance employee productivity, lower turnover, and increase customer satisfaction. But when employees become disengaged, they accomplish less and forfeit energy to negative behaviors that contribute to drag and further deplete morale. Research shows it takes three to five years for engagement to decline to its lowest point,[9] so, like Boutique Financial, compensating with excess energy can go unnoticed for years before barriers finally become apparent and take their toll.

On the basis of our research, we have identified the most common execution barriers that cause drag and how companies can orchestrate solutions to remove them. Specifically, chapters 3 through 6 distribute barriers and best practices for sustainable execution into "four shifts" and describe specific approaches to create a customized program of action toward a pathway for improvement. Also, proprietary to our book is the *Cost of Execution* (CO_x) factor explained in chapter 2. CO_x is a performance metric that organizations can use to measure the overall drag caused by barriers that obstruct the execution path forward and cause energy loss. Consistent with the idea that sustainable execution is a continuous regime or organizational practice, it is important that leadership have a measurement or key performance indicator (KPI) they can use to monitor improvements to their execution system. Finally, as sustainable execution is not a "how to" approach to driving results but a fundamental shift in mindset, identifying and empowering the right execution leaders can be a challenge. Part four concludes the book by describing three unique traits that differentiate execution leaders from other leaders in the organization and one trait so fatal it can derail execution. When all chapters are put into practice, organizations will improve their ability to execute by removing barriers and orchestrating solutions that drive short-term results and sustain longer-time performance.

2

COST OF EXECUTION (CO_x)

Many organizations have established a discipline for getting things done using best practices such as balanced scorecards, lean, and total quality management (TQM). The fundamental principles of *sustainable execution* explain why in some organizations these best practices for execution work well, while other organizations continue to struggle. To realize the best possible results, organizations need to stabilize the business to maintain and improve productivity while promoting flexibility to adjust to changes in the external environment. Similar to continuous improvement, or *kaizen*, sustainable execution is an incremental, flexible, and ongoing effort to fill execution gaps by reallocating resources, streamlining work, and reducing waste through better alignment of goals within an organization. However, sustainable execution is more holistic in that it brings to light the need to continuously reassess and remove barriers that distract the organization's ability to work across silos and focus energy on the most important goals and objectives. As such, making improvements to sustainable execution requires that organizations have a way to track and measure progress in achieving short-term results without impeding the long-term viability of the business.

The *Cost of Execution (CO_x)* factor is a key performance indicator (KPI) that organizations can use to monitor the effectiveness

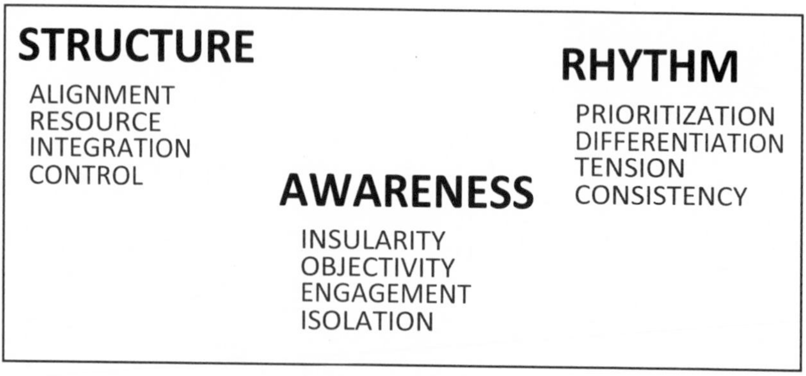

STRUCTURE		RHYTHM
STRUCTURE ALIGNMENT RESOURCE INTEGRATION CONTROL		**RHYTHM** PRIORITIZATION DIFFERENTIATION TENSION CONSISTENCY
	AWARENESS INSULARITY OBJECTIVITY ENGAGEMENT ISOLATION	

Figure 2.1 Sustainable Execution Barriers

of their execution system. It measures the overall drag caused by barriers that obstruct the execution path forward and cause energy loss. Our inter-professional team of academics and practitioners uncovered twelve deep-rooted execution barriers,[1] which range from ineffective use of resources and poor alignment to stifling collaboration and distracting employees with "busy" work. A complete list of barriers is provided in figure 2.1. The total number of execution barriers creating drag on progress and wearing down resources is needed to calculate the CO_x factor. To simplify the concept, if an organization identifies two execution barriers (2 barriers/12 barriers), their CO_x factor is .17, indicating that approximately two of ten key stakeholders may be blinded by their assumptions, or 17 per cent of workflows are not well aligned to incentives. If another company relatively equal in size and competing in the same industry identifies five execution barriers, their drag factor is .42, indicating approximately four of ten key stakeholders may be blinded by assumptions, or 42 per cent of workflows are not well aligned to incentives. Comparing execution systems using the CO_x factor provides a signal to one company that they are executing well and urgency for the other to make improvements.

As illustrated in the example above, the CO$_x$ factor is not intended to be used as an absolute. It is most effective when barriers are evaluated and compared across groups within the same organization or with other organizations that face similar competitive pressures (e.g., similar industry) or execution demands (e.g., pace of change). Through our research, we have found some interesting results that we share throughout the book. Perhaps most striking is that individuals at the highest level of the organization identify fewer and different barriers, compared with those identified by individuals in lower management or more operational roles. There is an inverse relationship between management position and the CO$_x$ factor; the average CO$_x$ factor amongst senior executives is .16, compared to .50 amongst lower-level managers and staff. This means the perceived drag from execution increases as you move down the organization. There are several explanations for this. First, senior leadership have different priorities and often lose sight of barriers that impede day-to-day operations. Second, lower levels of the organization uncover operational barriers that are impeding the day-to-day whirlwind of activity such as excess controls and over-processed workflows that create undue burdens. Third, they are also more inclined to be unclear about the organization's goals and objectives, as they are not directly involved in strategy discussions. As such, using the CO$_x$ factor helps managers across organizational levels look beyond their perspective and arrive at a common understanding of different execution realities. Our team uses CO$_x$ in the following ways:

1 To assess the overall CO$_x$ of the organization over time to identify barriers and measure the impact of execution improvements. Using CO$_x$ in this way is very effective when an organization is either planning for or already amidst a major transformation or

change, as a high CO_x factor impedes an organization's readiness for change. Before an organization embarks on any strategic initiative that fundamentally changes the way they do business, identifying and removing barriers is a good idea. The GEG example described later in this chapter provides a detailed explanation of this case.

2 To align organizations vertically by helping senior leadership ensure the path between intention (i.e., the plan) and implementation (i.e., the work) is short and shallow. Execution is highly dependent on the delegation of work and responsibility throughout the organization. This approach to using CO_x is the most popular in our consulting practice, as we use the CO_x tool to identify costly disconnection points. For example, senior leadership are often protected from the whole truth; if a project is slipping in schedule or exceeding budget, managers may tend to keep details quiet while they remain optimistic the project will recover. Using CO_x in this way helps close the gaps and remove distractions to bring intentions closer to the implementation of getting things done.

3 To compare lines of business across the organization and assess the effectiveness of their different execution approaches. For example, we worked with one organization that used CO_x to identify ways they could help IT deliver more effectively on the needs of the business. They also learned that IT perceived their CO_x factor to be lower (.20) than the rest of the business (.34). By realizing the discrepancy, parties worked more closely together to update practices and tools to suit the needs of the collective organization.

4 And finally, to assist those responsible for managing people (e.g., department, project, initiative) to assess their personal leadership effectiveness. Complementary to other methods (e.g., 360° review), senior leadership who use CO_x describe it as a

holistic approach to assess the structure and rhythm of their personal execution system, as well as to reflect and infuse awareness into their own leadership behaviors.

Before moving on, let's return to Boutique Financial from chapter 1 – the company that failed to execute an ambitious growth strategy. If they had implemented a KPI such as the CO$_x$ factor, there is a good chance they would have prevented the financial shortfall. To reiterate, directors expressed their concern multiple times, but the executive team invested little time and effort identifying and removing barriers. By the time the financial shortfall happened, their execution system has deteriorated so much that five directors had resigned. When we visited Boutique Financial in 2016, a few executives continued to marginalize the impact of execution barriers. They were impatient with discussions about potential cultural issues and did not want to rehash whether or not initial targets may have been too aggressive. It was not until we assessed the organization using CO$_x$ that an urgency to improve their execution system was established. We uncovered seven of twelve barriers; their drag was double the industry average. With a sense of urgency and a clear understanding of what barriers were most prevalent, Boutique Financial were ready to make improvements to their execution system.

Sustainable Execution Barriers

When organizations struggle to deliver results, the first reaction is to look for something that is missing. They look to a new strategy, a change in leadership, an adjustment to the organization chart, or additional resources as solutions. A continuous regimen of identifying barriers, making improvements, and reassessing barriers encourages organizations to rethink the comprehensiveness of their execution system by first addressing what is missing, but then diving deeper to remove distractions that are getting in the way. Figure 2.1 illustrates execution barriers across the structure, rhythm, and awareness execution levers. Once an organization understands where execution barriers are impeding performance, they can address the ones that matter most and lower their cost of execution.

Structural barriers impede execution, as they interfere with how resources are allocated, day-to-day work aligns with the strategy, and incentives influence productive behavior. A strong execution structure is needed to make difficult budget trade-offs and effectively cascade goals, objectives, and metrics to all levels of the organization so that the entire organization is clear about goals to achieve, how to achieve them, and why they are important. Even if you are a well-established firm operating in a stable industry, having structural barriers can be extremely problematic. In fact, a landmark study by the Harris Poll in 2012 reported only 51 per cent of employees truly understand what *they* need to do to help the organization achieve its goals.[2] Effective structure is needed for organizations to help people understand how to adjust their day-to-day work to adapt to changes in strategy and direction. Structural barriers include:

- **Resource Barrier:** Resources are not sufficiently allocated to the most important priorities as the result of affordability or protectionism, and that creates a perception of insufficient resources, or resources being caught in unproductive uses.
- **Alignment Barrier:** People do not understand what they need to do and why what they do is important for achieving the most important goals and objectives.
- **Integration Barrier:** The right information is not available at the right place and time because people are overloaded with data, they are resistant to using a new system, or the tools do not provide the functionality they really need.

- **Control Barrier:** Organizational policies, procedures, and control systems are either underdeveloped such that undue risk is incurred, or excessive such that undue burden is created.

Rhythm barriers impede the organization's ability to accelerate execution and pivot smoothly when the need arises. Strong rhythm is needed in order to be productive, day in and day out, and focus energy on the right priorities. A good rhythm is evident in the way employees work. It is heightened by creating a healthy pressure to perform through a sense of urgency and competition as well as training and honing processes to increase consistency. Rhythm provides the momentum for agility and responsiveness and is essential for executing efficiently in more dynamic environments. Rhythm barriers include:

- **Tension Barrier:** The need to pursue competing organizational objectives (e.g., quality and efficiency) results in unhealthy trade-offs. Either tension is lacking, causing valuable resources to be wasted, or there is too much tension, resulting in valuable resources being exhausted or burnt out.
- **Consistency Barrier:** Failure to establish discipline through standardized work, a regime of training and development that infuses practice, and/or ineffective management of vocabulary and terminology cause quality problems and inefficient day-to-day work.
- **Differentiation Barrier:** "Playing safe" interferes with execution because organizations fail to provide feedback and/or have difficult conversations, allowing poor performers (i.e., products, services, and employees) to consume valuable resources and generate limited return.
- **Prioritization Barrier:** Priorities are vastly under-communicated, resulting in people focusing on urgent distractions or work that suits their individual needs instead of what helps the organization meet its goals.

Awareness barriers impede the organization's ability to "pay attention" to what's really going on and take appropriate action. These barriers are essential to understanding the full scope of sustainable execution; however, they are often overlooked or marginalized, compared to other barriers, as they can be difficult for leadership to see. Nonetheless, awareness levers are needed to foster an execution culture built on trust and accountability. Don Sull and Charles Spinosa claim execution is most effective when managed as a *"dynamic network of promises,"*[3] as holding people accountable is less productive than empowering people to *be accountable* to the commitments they have made. Awareness is evident when careful listening and open-mindedness are everyday practice. Whether your organization is well established or a new start-up, biased decision-making, silo mentality, and insularity will quietly eat away at your ability to execute. Awareness barriers include:

- **Engagement Barrier:** Employees, customers, and other stakeholders lack the motivation, passion, and commitment to achieve the organization's goals and objectives.
- **Objectivity Barrier:** Most often manifested in the decision-making process, lack of objectivity creates unjustified delays, misunderstanding about "how" decisions are made, and skepticism due to bias and politics.
- **Isolation Barrier:** Ineffective management of cultural and geographic differences (e.g., time zone, language barriers) and/or allowing "silo" thinking and insider "cliques" will silence innovation and harm cooperation and collaboration.
- **Insularity Barrier:** Deep-rooted assumptions and perspectives trap organizations in their past experience and prevent them from critically assessing risks and new relevant information.

Assessing the Cost of Execution (CO$_x$)

Adopting a measurable value or KPI for execution such as the CO$_x$ factor allows organizations to gain a comprehensive understanding of how a positive outcome was actually achieved. Just because an organization meets their quarterly targets or delivers a project on time and budget does not mean they achieved results through a productive path or whirlwind of activity. Assessing the CO$_x$ factor may uncover the reality that the activity behind the positive outcome was actually more synonymous to a destructive vortex than a productive whirlwind. The first step in assessing CO$_x$ is to identify the barriers that cause energy loss along the path to success. Working through each barrier, organizations may evaluate:

- Are resources being used in unproductive ways?
- Are targets too aggressive that compliance or quality trade-offs are being made?
- Are mandatory and/or fragmented policies and procedures across departments resulting in counterproductive work?
- Is productivity being sufficiently monitored to create healthy pressure to perform?
- Are the most important decisions being addressed in a timely manner?
- Is decision-making unbiased and objective?
- Are valuable skills, expertise, and knowledge underutilized as the result of language barriers and cultural differences?

It is important to highlight that over the years some organizations have questioned the legitimacy of CO$_x$ because it is a measure of individual perspectives and perceptions. Admittedly, how each individual perceives the existence of barriers is heavily influenced by personal experiences and biases. However, organizations are encouraged to consider each perspective as a data point about the organization's execution reality. In other words, every perspective influences the overall culture for getting things done. Like any data set, there will be outliers that organizations can choose to ignore or probe as a leading indicator of a potential risk.

It is also important to recognize that CO_x is a subjective measure; identifying a barrier does not always equate to a problem with the way things are being done. Overbearing metrics do not necessarily mean metrics need to be removed. It may simply mean the organization needs to do a better job of explaining why metrics are needed and what they are being used for. Biased decision-making does not mean the decision process needs to be more objective; it may mean decision-making needs to be more transparent so people understand why certain decisions are being made. In summary, the CO_x factor helps organizations identify opportunities to improve their execution system as well as eliminate distractions that impede how things are done.

Table 2.1 is a summary of CO_x results for a retail organization, Games and Entertainment Galore (GEG),[4] we worked with in 2014. They engaged our help as their industry was undergoing significant change due to increased competition from online retailers. Customer expectations were changing and, as a traditional "bricks and mortar" retailer, they needed to improve their supply chain to better coordinate service across the online and in-store business units to provide customers with a more seamless and consistent experience. GEG relied most on structural levers to execute. They used formal, structural methods of resource allocation, hierarchical authority, rules, and policies to guide behavior. They also had sophisticated enterprise systems that integrated data and standardized work processes across functions of the business.

Assessment Overview: We identified six specific barriers that were creating a drag in progress and straining resources, as evident by the higher-than-industry-average CO_x factor (.50). The

Table 2.1 CO$_x$ Assessment for GEG

Execution levers	Barriers of sustainable execution	
Structure: high	Control barrier	
Rhythm: low	Tension, consistency, and prioritization barriers	
Awareness: moderate	Objectivity and isolation barriers	
Overall execution performance	Sustainability score: low	CO$_x$: .50 > .32 average

sustainability score was also low, alerting GEG to the fact that employees felt the company was struggling to keep up with market demand and make changes "stick." The short-term demands to go online and streamline in-store business processes were impeding longer-term customer experience and loyalty. To our surprise, the financial performance of the company remained healthy, and so we asked, "To what degree do you think your ability to sustain performance to date is due to your industry position? If you were smaller in size and revenue, could you sustain bumps and bruises to the same degree?" This was a pivotal point in the assessment, as it allowed us to draw attention to the fact that the company's deep pockets may be compensating for execution barriers. For the most part, the senior leadership team was confident the company could return to what made them great at one time; however, directors and managers were less convinced about the long-term sustainability of the company. They knew the organization was not responding to customer needs, and barriers related to internal politics and outdated policies and procedures were impeding change and improvement.

Before moving on to the next section, it is important to note that our team worked with this organization for a six-month period, so attempting to explain how we helped lower their CO$_x$ and describe the specific recommendations that guided their pathway for improvement in a few short pages is not easy. If the next section gets complicated, we encourage readers to continuously revisit table 2.1, as recalling how GEG's six barriers relate to the three execution levers will be very helpful for following along.

Lowering the Cost of Execution (CO$_x$)

Looking at the barriers across the execution levers, we analyzed the capability of structure, rhythm, and awareness to help us *orchestrate the balancing act*. Only one barrier in structure and three in rhythm was not surprising, considering they had been in business for over sixty years, they were large in size and accustomed to operating in a relatively slow-moving industry. However, their high structure and low rhythm was not the right balance to support the change to online retailing. Like other traditional brick-and-mortar retailers, execution by structure left them scrambling to respond faster to market changes and new customer opportunities.

Although we were inclined to recommend they start by turning down structure, we needed to do more analysis to determine which barrier to eliminate first. Through our experience we've learned that action to remove barriers coalesces around four "shifts" that provide a pragmatic approach to implementing changes to lower CO$_x$ and improve sustainability. Each shift is unique, as it unleashes

Table 2.2 "Shifts" and Execution Barriers

	Capacity shift	Alignment shift	Collaboration shift	Focus shift
Energy source	Source energy to build capacity	Align energy to generate momentum	Share energy to promote synergy	Ground energy to sustain focus
Structure	Resource barrier	Alignment barrier	Integration barrier	Control barrier
Rhythm	Tension barrier	Consistency barrier	Differentiation barrier	Prioritization barrier
Awareness	Engagement barrier	Objectivity barrier	Isolation barrier	Insularity barrier
	Filling gaps		Removing distractions	

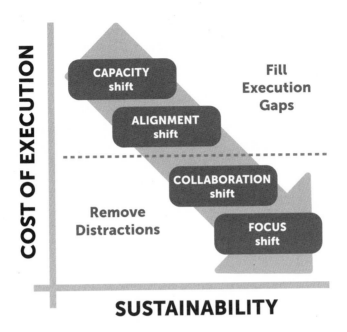

COST OF EXECUTION

CAPACITY
shift

Fill
Execution
Gaps

ALIGNMENT
shift

COLLABORATION
shift

Remove
Distractions

FOCUS
shift

SUSTAINABILITY

Figure 2.2 Shift-to-Execute Framework

an energy source by building capacity, generating momentum, promoting synergy, or sustaining focus. As illustrated in table 2.2, there is a natural progression of activity from left to right, starting in the lightest column and moving through to the darkest column. This progression is summarized in the Shift-to-Execute framework (figure 2.2) that illustrates the pathway for improvement that lowers the CO$_x$ and improves sustainability. Inherent in this progression is the need to stabilize a backbone for execution by *filling gaps* BEFORE *removing distractions* so the organization can pursue flexible ways to accelerate work and adjust to changes in the environment. Using this framework, we identified the first step for GEG was to address their tension, consistency, and objectivity barriers to stabilize their

backbone before removing distractions caused by control, prioritization, and isolation. Before explaining how we made improvements, it is important to explain filling gaps, removing distractions,
and orchestrating balance.

Filling the Execution Gaps. To get started, organizations need
to address barriers that exist because something is *inherently out-
of-place or missing* from the execution backbone. The *Capacity Shift*
requires that there are sufficient resources to meet the company's
goals, that resources are allocated across competing objectives, and
that gaps in incentives and rewards are filled to enhance engagement and drive value. For example, if a new initiative is deemed
important in the organization's strategy but insufficient resources
are allocated, execution on that initiative will likely fail. A dra-
matic reallocation of resources provides a clear message about
what is important and what is not. The *Alignment Shift* addresses
gaps in the definition of goals, objectives, tactics, and metrics
to make sure the organization is pursuing a common direction
through consistent and objective day-to-day practice. Behavioral
change requires that people throughout the organization are clear
about what they need to do, how to do it, and why it is important.
When clear goals and objectives are missing or under-communicated, people waste time and energy working hard on things that
matter less.

Removing Distractions. Once essential execution elements are in
place, organizations can start eliminating barriers that disable execution by *getting in the way*. The *Collaboration Shift* removes information barriers by leveraging data and analytics as well as reducing
internal politics to make better business decisions and encourage
the organization to take appropriate risks. When organizations are
exploring new terrain, barriers in collaboration can quickly take
them off track and into wasteful territory. Also increased uncertainty can make organizations skeptical and deplete trust if business

units are hesitant to come out of their silos to help each other out. The *Focus Shift* adjusts internal controls and establishes clear priorities to minimize distraction from busy work and/or personal agendas. Prioritization is important, as it helps companies focus on what is most important, which is imperative when redirecting energy to new initiatives. Finally, leadership needs to be open to new, relevant information to keep execution on track and mitigate risk. Many organizations put all of their execution energy into filling the gaps and wonder why they continue to be out-performed. To sustain performance, organizations need to remove distractions to transform from "protecting what is" to exploring and exploiting "what could be." Once distractions are removed, they can focus their energy on what is most important.

Orchestrating Balance. Navigating each shift requires an orchestration of structure, rhythm, and awareness. Let's examine how GEG would navigate the focus shift, as it is good illustration of how orchestration works. As the company was constrained by two barriers in this shift (i.e., control and prioritization barriers), focus was clearly a problem, but they could not simply remove controls that were outdated or burdensome to make improvements. Orchestration requires that controls be prioritized, as they are put in place for a reason. Removing them has consequences that need to be considered initially and monitored continuously over time. A shift in focus would also need to consider any assumptions about why, how, and by whom controls were originally put in place. If a control on the chopping block was put in place by the CEO, removing it without clear justification and communication could have significant consequences. As GEG did not suffer from an insularity barrier, getting leadership to critically assess risks and new information would likely not be a problem; however, getting their acceptance was still required. In many ways, orchestrating shifts across structure, rhythm, and awareness levers is consistent with best practices in managing change. We've found organizations that navigate shifts and remove barriers using this approach are more capable of making change "stick," as the approach embeds the change into the day-to-day routine of the organization and emphasizes the importance of buy-in and acceptance.

Making Improvements at GEG

Leadership's initial inclination was to address the control barrier; they felt an adjustment in policies and procedures was needed to support their expectation to become more agile. As GEG was used to executing by structure, our team was not surprised. However, we explained that eventually controls would need to be adjusted, but the company had some gaps in their execution backbone that they needed to address first. We explained that tension, consistency, and objectivity barriers were preventing their investment in flexible, agile tools and techniques from being infused into day-to-day work. Improved rhythm and awareness would discourage people from reverting to the old way of doing things. We recommended the following actions to the leadership team:

- Spend more time and energy providing oversight and feedback on the adoption and use of agile tools and techniques. We explained that as people venture into new ways of doing day-to-day work, tension emerges between the old and new ways of doing things. Evidence of oversight and regular feedback is needed to reassure employees that leadership values the change.
- Create an innate, shared understanding of what the organization means by "agility." Even though becoming more

agile was a popular trend in modern business practices, the meaning of the word was ill-defined and ambiguous. As GEG used the word *agility* to set a new direction for the company, establishing a clear definition and common vocabulary was important.

- Finally, we tried to inform leadership about the objectivity barrier, but they were quick to marginalize it. They explained, "Our company has undergone significant changes in terms of how we make decisions, but everything can't go their way." GEG had improved their decision practices to be more transparent and broadly influenced, but one manager described the change as an *"exercise in effort"* – time and energy wasted as managers were simply being put through the motion of being involved, but had little to no influence actual decisions made. After further investigation, we agreed with leadership – decisions were more informed; however, feedback was not being provided, so managers did not understand how decisions were being made. So managers needed to do a better job of communicating back.

Once GEG had filled their execution gaps, the next set of recommendations was to eliminate barriers that were getting in the way.

- We started by turning leadership attention to customer feedback to justify the possibility that unhealthy competition between the online and in-store business had created an isolation barrier that was causing the company to fall short in their efforts to deliver customer value. As these groups had worked together in the past, leadership assumed they would figure out how to coordinate efforts. Managers explained that ultimately the customers were paying the price, and there were many complaints about the disconnect between shopping through the online channel and in-store services. Leadership agreed to explore the working relationship between divisions, and they understood the need to handle the situation delicately. They planned to have one-on-one conversations with key stakeholders from both divisions and commissioned experts from the human resource department to explore potential issues.

- Next, we helped GEG inventory eighty-four organizational controls, policies, and procedures and helped them realize their traditional use of control was counterintuitive to rebalancing to a more agile approach. Many controls were outdated, and overbearing reporting, compliance, quality control, and performance metrics created burden on day-to-day productivity. Also new management approaches (e.g., flexible budgets, lean management) had introduced new controls but none were taken away. One particular story caught our attention. A customer had pre-ordered five dolls – one doll for each member of the popular band One Direction. To the customer's surprise, the order arrived on multiple days and each individual doll came in an excessively large box packed to the brim with polystyrene packing peanuts. This customer experience was not unique – there were hundreds of comments from customers expressing similar frustration. The warehouse managers explained how the new order system predetermined the size of box for each order as a way to control packaging costs. Warehouse productivity was evaluated on the basis of compliance between packaging material and order fulfillment, so even when employees recognized the opportunity to use better judgment they were given the incentive to adhere to the system's recommendation. To be more responsive, GEG needed to evaluate, update, and lean out their organizational controls so people had the time, energy, and flexibility needed to process exceptions and adapt appropriately to customer demands. We encouraged them to orchestrate this change by prioritizing each control according to the burden as well as the degree to which eliminating controls would create undue risk. Fourteen organizational controls (17 per cent) were removed.

Four months after we made our recommendations, our team received a call from GEG. They wanted to discuss the isolation barrier, as they believed they had uncovered the source. Leadership had done their "deep dive" to explore what was really going on and learned that the online business felt strongly the company was not making difficult financial trade-offs to supply them with resources they needed to succeed. They were the business unit that was ripe for growth, but in-store had become accustomed to having access to surplus. Leadership were concerned this would create additional friction between departments – this was the issue they wanted to discuss. We validated their concern but reminded them a shift in capacity was essential to the backbone for execution, so if leadership agreed this was the best approach, they needed to alter budget allocations as soon as possible.

One Year Later

Our team revisited GEG in early 2016 to assess improvements to their execution system. Updated results are illustrated in table 2.3. Overall, they removed two execution barriers (reduced CO$_x$ by .17) and slightly improved sustainability. The leadership had delivered on their commitment to improve rhythm by providing effective oversight and feedback and reassuring employees that their efforts to move to Agile[5] day-to-day practices was indeed important and highly valued. The removal of fourteen controls eliminated the structural control barrier, and the objectivity barrier was also eliminated as middle managers had become more aware about how

Table 2.3 Results for GEG (One Year Later)

Execution levers	Barriers of sustainable execution
Structure: no change	Resource barrier
Rhythm: higher	Consistency and prioritization barriers
Awareness: higher	Isolation barrier
Overall execution performance	Sustainability: slight improvement CO_x: .33 > .32 average

decisions were being made. Improvements reduced drag and made a slight improvement in sustainability, indicating the company was on the right track in responding to market forces and improving customer satisfaction.

Despite efforts to standardize and clarify vocabulary related to the Agile approach, a consistency barrier was still evident. So more work was needed to establish a regime for Agile training and development. Also GEG's attempt to remove the isolation barrier had some unfortunate yet expected consequences on structure as a resource barrier emerged. The in-store line of business was frustrated by changes made to supply the online business with more resources and were struggling to find efficiencies to accommodate budget cuts. We explained that GEG effectively orchestrated the resource allocation, as neither a tension nor engagement barrier emerged; however, they would need to continue to remove isolation distractions, as the new allocation added fuel to the fire between departments. The good news was that the leadership was aware of the strain and equated it to a cost associated with navigating through turbulent times. They remained confident that investing in their online business was a difficult step in the right direction.

Sustainable Execution Diagnostic Assessment (SEDA)

Now that you have an understanding of the CO_x factor, it is important to mention that we have translated our experience into a quantitative assessment tool we call the Sustainable Execution Diagnostic Assessment, or SEDA. A comprehensive description and access to this tool is available at www.sustainableexecution.ca. In general the tool assists organizations by providing a way to quantify sustainability as well as a comprehensive approach to evaluating barriers to determine the CO$_x$ factor. Specifically, a predictive model was created using regression analysis on how all twelve execution barriers affect capacity, alignment, collaboration, and focus. The degree of influence for each barrier is determined by weight (or co-efficient) that represents its overall impact on drag. SEDA also allows organizations to identify the most salient execution barriers and evaluate the capability of structure, rhythm, and awareness levers to orchestrate the balancing act. It is based on a standard questionnaire that has been administered over 1,500 times in our research. Though the online tool is helpful in quantifying the CO$_x$ factor and comparing results within and across industries, readers can conduct a qualitative assessment of barriers and estimate their sustainability and CO$_x$ factor by working through the following chapters.

PART TWO

Filling the Gaps

Each chapter in part two and part three outlines a different approach, or shift, that optimizes a specific source or use of energy to improve sustainability and lower the cost of execution. Designed from our research, each shift addresses a different set of barriers from across the structure, rhythm, and awareness spectrum.

Customizing Your Pathway for Improvement. Readers do not need to work through chapters 3 through 6 in sequence. Each was written to stand alone so readers are able to proceed directly to the chapter that is most applicable to their pathway for improvement. Knowing where to start depends on what execution barriers are most prevalent in your execution system.

- Chapter 3: *Resource, tension,* and *engagement* barriers that create energy gaps needed to build capacity.
- Chapter 4: *Alignment, consistency,* and *objectivity* barriers that create gaps needed to generate momentum.
- Chapter 5: *Integration, differentiation,* and *isolation* barriers that distract and divert energy away from promoting synergy.
- Chapter 6: *Control, prioritization,* and *insularity* barriers that distract and divert energy away from sustaining focus.

In customizing your pathway for improvement, remember to *fill gaps* before *removing distractions*, as explained in our Shift-to-Execute framework (figure 2.2). Orchestrating solutions that fill gaps in capacity (chapter 3) and momentum (chapter 4) will make sure elements essential to the backbone of the execution system are in place. Readers who are confident they have no gaps in their execution backbone may wish to skip these chapters and proceed directly to the last two shifts. Synergy (chapter 5) and focus (chapter 6) explore ways organizations can orchestrate solutions that *remove distractions* to conserve energy, to enhance productivity and optimize performance.

Sustainable Execution Diagnostic Assessment (SEDA)

Readers using SEDA as an online supplement to the book will notice the orchestration of structure, rhythm, and awareness for each shift is illustrated using a wind turbine analogy.

- Structural barriers are illustrated by the *tower height, construction, and position*. For example, towers that are too short or have damaged or missing blades impede the organization's ability to supply and use energy.
- Rhythm barriers interfere with the *spin of the turbine blades*. When the spin is intermittent or stopped, energy cannot be supplied or used.
- *Clouds and sun* illustrate the organization's ability to supply and use renewable sources of energy (i.e., wind and solar). When barriers interfere with objectivity and employee engagement, winds reduce and clouds emerge that block energy from the sun.

Finally, the tool can also be used to customize your pathway for improvement. It uses regression analysis to calculate a score for each of the four shifts, based on the severity[1] of each barrier. Again, scores are not intended to be used as absolutes; they simply provide organizations with a way to determine the shift (or chapter) where improvement is most likely to lower the cost of execution and improve sustainability.

3

SHIFT RESOURCES TO
BUILD CAPACITY

When asked what would improve an organization's ability to execute, the most common answer is *"more money and people."* The problem is that today's companies face tighter financial constraints, so more money and people are seldom an option. Very few organizations can afford to have resources stuck in unproductive uses. This requires organizations to find innovative ways to stretch and redistribute existing resources as well as identify new sources of energy to deliver results. Shifting resources to build capacity orchestrates an energy system that is capable of *doing more with less*. This does not mean employees need to work harder; it means organizations need to make the best use of their resources and find productive ways to motivate employees, partners, and even customers to dedicate time and attention to achieving results. The "do more with less" challenge is virtually everywhere – companies across every industry including government and not-for-profit organizations are expected to minimize waste and prevent over-spending. As such, this chapter explains different ways organizations can shift resources to establish a backbone for building capacity and do more with less as a result.

Many companies can generate extra or "burst" capacity for short periods to chase down deadlines and/or address unexpected challenges. In sustainable execution, extra short-term energy is like an adrenaline rush where productivity is enhanced by people working overtime hours under stressful conditions. The problem with adrenaline is the negative long-term consequences such as stress, anxiety, and burnout when used too much. A 2016 study reported 95 per cent of human resource executives agree employee burnout is sabotaging their workforce.[1] The three culprits according to the study are unfair compensation, unreasonable workload, and too much overtime/after-hours work. The problem is that in the face of fewer resources and higher demands, organizations feel there is little they can do about these issues. In sustainable execution, solutions can be found by building greater long-term capacity for performance.

Through our research, we learned that organizations and industries build long-term capacity in different ways. For example, the retail industry has been building capacity for decades by finding new ways to delight customers while simultaneously implementing creative solutions to reduce costs. Resources are allocated where they drive the greatest value, often requiring difficult financial trade-offs between customer service resources and technological automation. For example, investments in self-checkout and order kiosks are essential for reducing cost but need to be carefully designed so customers derive value in using them. Self-service allows customers to place their own orders, which not only reduces errors, but increases capacity to fulfill a greater number of orders with the same staff. Long-term capacity for performance in retail also comes from delighting customers; loyalty programs that leverage data and analytics build the organization's capacity to please customers through personalized offers and valuable product discounts. When delighted customers jump to social media to recommend a product or service to their friends, retailers increase their capacity to generate revenue with lower advertising investment.

In health care, radical shifts in budget are forcing the industry as a whole to find ways to provide care for an aging population with fewer resources. Similar to retail, data and analytics build capacity to empower patients through personalized care and advances in data-driven diagnosis. In this industry, however, trading off care provided by doctors and nurses for technological automation brings along more risk. Innovative digital solutions such as actionable intelligence[2] and advanced triage systems[3] increase the capacity of doctors and hospitals to care for a growing number of patients requiring acute care by authorizing nurses and other providers in the patient's circle of care to diagnosis issues and make decisions. Programs such as home dialysis and tele-health monitoring[4] increase the capacity of patients and their families to self-manage and fill gaps in care while lessening the demand for more costly hospital services.

Although the two industries build capacity in different ways, there are some similarities. This chapter explains these similarities by exposing relevant execution barriers and providing ways organizations can improve their execution system by filling execution gaps to build capacity.

What Is Capacity?

Bain & Co. conducted a study of 2,000 companies over ten years and found that only 10 per cent achieved sustained, profitable growth.[5] The capability that set winners apart was the ability to source capacity in more innovative ways. Eighty-five per cent of those winners moved far beyond mere cost-cutting to explore ways they can leverage external resources and bring new products to market faster. Novel in today's digital era is building capacity through new business models that transform customer experiences and internal capabilities using digital technologies. Retail self-service and tele-health monitoring are examples of building capacity in this way. Take, for example, a patient with chronic obstructive pulmonary disease who monitors his own vitals using tele-monitoring technology. Daily oxygen saturation, weight, and heart rate readings are logged on a personal care website that the patient and immediate family can monitor. Doctors, nurses, and other health professionals are provided with new incentives to empower the family with information so they become a new source of energy that enhances continuous care for the patient. In this example, energy supply increases through more efficient and effective use of resources (people and money), innovative practices that leverage external resources (i.e., patients, families), and incentives that motivate and inspire people to take initiative and "go the extra mile." As illustrated in figure 3.1, our research found three primary capabilities for shifting resources to build capacity.

Energy supply starts by making sure the *right resources (money, people, time) are allocated to the right job.* Careful management of budget, portfolio, workforce, and schedule are all essential to optimizing how, where, and when work gets done. Organizations also need to make bold decisions and significant budget changes when necessary. Take, for example, the decision made by Ford CEO Jim Hackett in May 2018 to shed $5 billion from capital spending by cutting most of its North American car lineup to unleash resources needed to capitalize on emerging opportunities essential for survival. Building capacity also requires organizations to ensure work is assigned to the person best suited to do the job at the right level of the organization. When people are accountable and compensated to do work below their pay grade, the overall capacity of the organization decreases. Finally, when people fail to appropriately delegate work, their capacity to do what they are actually paid to do also decreases. According to a 2012 study by Physicians Foundation, physicians spend nearly 22 per cent of their time on non-clinical paperwork.

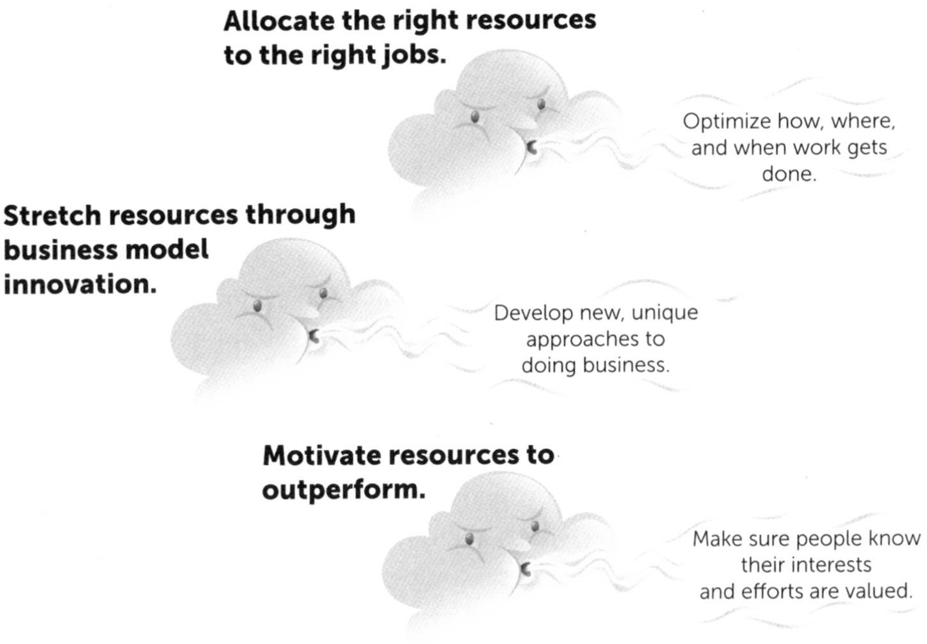

**Allocate the right resources
to the right jobs.**

Optimize how, where,
and when work gets
done.

**Stretch resources through
business model
innovation.**

Develop new, unique
approaches to
doing business.

**Motivate resources to
outperform.**

Make sure people know
their interests
and efforts are valued.

Figure 3.1 Sustainable Execution Approach to Shift Resources

Many of those have staff who handle finances and other aspects of the business, but they either do not take time to effectively delegate work or have a hard time letting go of control.[6]

Next, organizations need to find novel ways to unleash potential sources of energy caught up in business processes that are tired or outdated. When resources are *stretched through business model innovation*, the energy release is like letting go of a stretched rubber band to amplify capacity and do more with less. Business model innovation is the development of new, unique approaches to doing business by encouraging people to challenge fundamental business assumptions that define the status quo. Organizations have been building capacity in this way for decades, with examples such as Southwest Airlines' ten-minute turnaround initiative dating back to 1972. However, the potential for business model innovation has recently accelerated as the result of advances in digital technology. Unlike humans, computers work twenty-four hours a day at optimized performance, doing work of millions of people in a single second.[7] Digital analyst and author Brian Solis describes today's potential for business model innovation as "the end of business as usual" and claims disruptive technology requires businesses fundamentally adapt or die. Process optimization is being accelerated by analytics, and artificial intelligence is processing information faster and more efficiently than humans. Social and mobile technologies are empowering the "crowd"[8] to contribute time, energy, and ideas. Amazon Go is a great example, as their stores are devoid of cashiers and registers. Shoppers make purchases seamlessly and leave without even pausing to pull out their credit card. Innovations such as cashierless convenience are extraordinary. Not only do they save time and extend the availability of 24/7 convenience, they also increase capacity to deal with age-old problems such as detecting fraud and reducing theft.

Finally, energy comes from a positive work environment that is **motivated to out-perform** expectations. This energy source is most challenging to manage because it is discretionary. It is very powerful when people rise up to the challenge but if they do not, capacity is dramatically reduced. Perhaps most challenging is that getting the right resources to the right job and changes to business models can push organizations to new realities that bring them out of their comfort zone. Incentives that motivate people to out-perform expectations and reward their efforts are definitely important. However, only 40 per cent of respondents in our research were engaged by incentives, compared to 87 per cent who agreed that motivation accelerated performance when incentives were supported by leadership's willingness to give them a pat on the back and make them feel appreciated. As such, additional capacity arises when all stakeholders in an organization's broader ecosystem (i.e., employees, partners, and customers) feel their interests and discretionary efforts are valued. Organizations should not overlook the importance of personal recognition and public "thank yous" when building capacity. A positive work environment does not remove authority; in fact a firmer approach may be necessary at times, as reallocating resources and taking people out of their comfort zone is not easy. The key to positive motivation is recognizing that expectations for performance need to be achievable,[9] and authoritative approaches have longer-term consequences when they are overused. Senior executives capable of leading the organization, motivating performance beyond expectation, and expressing their appreciation all at the same time raise capacity to its peak.

Barriers to Building Capacity

Barriers to building capacity reflect mediocrity or complacency in the way resources are allocated and the way people work. In sustainable execution, complacency is the dangerous force that diminishes capacity. Voices in the company that create urgency for new ideas and innovation get buried in hierarchy, and the need to meet short-term profitability goals overshadows long-term viability. Our research found that companies experiencing rapid change were 87 per cent effective at building capacity, compared to 67 per cent in slower, more stable organizations. However, even rapidly changing organizations may allow complacency to seep in without their noticing. Failing to shift resources to explore new opportunities and mitigate potential hazards is an internal epidemic that, some experts claim, irrevocably maimed companies such as Kodak[10] and BlackBerry.[11] Our sustainable execution model highlights three barriers that prevent organizations from shifting resources to build capacity.

Resource Barrier

When a resource barrier is uncovered in an organization, the common reason given is affordability. Specifically, "We could execute more effectively if we had more money and people." When this is truly the case, the problem in our sustainable execution model is not actually a resource barrier, it is a deficiency in alignment, which will be discussed further in chapter 4. Resource barriers in our model emanate from two common problems. First, highly controlled, annual financial budget planning processes are prone to *resources getting caught in unproductive uses* that represent waste. In sustainable execution, every line item on a budget needs to be analyzed regularly to justify needs and costs. In fact, we found resources allocated to stable, established lines of business are often most complacent in stretching resources to their limit. Every line of business will benefit when they set expectations that push performance limits. Organizations also need to consider transforming budgeting from an annual one-time planning exercise to an ongoing practice that enables resources to remain somewhat fluid so they can continuously redirect energy to where it is needed most. Second, budget planning often removes contingency and excess reserves to the point that *resource availability is too tight*. Doing more with less does not equate to fewer people being required to do more work. Resources need to be stretched to generate the most value; however, there is a point of diminishing returns that organizations should not exceed.

In our experience, detecting resource barriers is not always easy. They are most commonly recognized through the following side effects:

- *Responsibility overload* pushes resources to a breaking point and causes productivity to suffer. In our research, we discovered that an alarming 68 per cent of senior managers admit to asking their employees to take on too many additional responsibilities as a result of insufficient resources.
- *Stifled innovation* occurs as people have little time to think about ways they can do their job more effectively. Companies such as 3M, Google, and HP Inc. build slack into their execution environment by allowing employees to spend up to 15 per cent of their time experimenting with new ideas[12] – in fact, 3M scientist Art Fry envisioned the now iconic Post-it Note during his 15 per cent time.[13]
- A *resistance to failure* versus a *"fail and correct" approach* may increase the risk of financial shortfall in the long run. Any company attempting to compete in today's complex digital era needs to give employees the freedom and resources to try new approaches. A culture that doesn't encourage experimentation and tolerate failure will struggle to find its way.
- *Quality problems* arise from cost-cutting through reduced investment in requirements identification, testing, and training. Any organization that has experienced a significant technology implementation understands that dollars invested in technology are minimal, compared to the investment made in implementation. Resources are needed for improvement and adapting to change through investments in experimentation, collaboration, and knowledge sharing.

Tension Barrier

Execution excellence is rarely found along the path of least resistance, as it is difficult to make progress on seemingly competing objectives at the same time. For example, every leader knows that maximizing quality and increasing profit margin on a product or service is not easy to do. Dollars invested in managing quality need to stretch to make sure profit margins are protected, and cost-saving initiatives must not impede the quality of the customer experience. In sustainable execution, the day-to-day rhythm capable of delivering on competing objectives is defined as *healthy tension*. When it exists, everyone in the organization is acutely aware of "doing more" to drive revenue, satisfy customers, improve quality, etc., "with fewer" resources.

There are two types of tension barriers. In the first, *tension is lacking, causing valuable resources to be wasted.* The day-to-day rhythm of activity lacks a sense of urgency, reflecting complacency in the way people approach their work. Without a sense of urgency, organizations lose sight of the fact that the speed of execution matters on all fronts, including revenue generation, product delivery, recruitment, customer service, and decision-making. Failure to act promptly results in opportunities lost, customer dissatisfaction, and other impacts that harm productivity and performance. The good news from our research is that 70 per cent of organizations agree that monitoring financial resources (i.e., cash flow, profitability) creates a healthy tension for performance by creating pressure to perform. The bad news is that only 26 per cent of organizations agree that day-to-day business processes are infused with healthy tension – processes are either lacking or so prescribed that activity focuses more on adherence to process than achieving desired results. Process optimization can certainly address a tension barrier; however, we offer the following advice when putting a process in place:

- Make people aware of related activities outside of the process so they are not overlooked.
- Monitor the process to identify sub-optimal choices that may be justified by process and make necessary adjustments.
- Evaluate the use of process in day-to-day activity to make sure it does not stifle communication and innovation.

We also found dependence on process can be problematic when it causes valuable resources to be wasted; 67 per cent of organizations agree that overwhelming use of "process" depletes healthy tension. Process prescribes work in ways that make it easy to measure, train people, monitor activity, and integrate work across departments but becomes problematic when it gets too rigid. When an execution system is burdened by process, getting approvals and working through procedure causes valuable resources to be wasted. As such, organizations are encouraged to explore alternative ways to establish healthy tension in day-to-day work. Daily check-ins and imposing deadlines are very effective in establishing a sense of urgency. Making a commitment to timely communication and feedback as well as clear meeting agendas are ways to keep things moving and send a message that other people's work is important. Finally, putting "hard numbers on time" infuses a sense of urgency by connecting time with money. Imagine if meetings were assigned a planned and actual budget to quantify value generated compared to time invested. We have infused this practice in a number of organizations and found when people connect time with money, meetings start on time, finish on time, and the thirty- or sixty-minute duration standard is tailored on the basis of the specific agenda items.

In the second type of tension barrier, *too much tension causes valuable resources to be exhausted or burnt out.* To reiterate, working under high-stress conditions is productive in small doses; short-term "burst" energy helps teams chase down a deadline or deal with an unexpected crisis. Tension barriers arise when the nature of day-to-day work puts a demand on resources that is so tense the execution system as a whole starts to break down. In some cases, the source of too much tension is unrealistic goals, but we found this to be secondary to the inability of organizations to establish *clear boundaries* that help workers understand their individual roles and responsibilities. Only 23 per cent of people in our study agreed their organization takes time to adjust specific roles and respon-sibilities to meet the changing demands of the business. Without boundaries, responsibility becomes blurred and energy is wasted on redundant efforts. Boundaries are also needed to help people make important trade-offs when faced with competing objectives. A good example of a boundary is a clear service agreement that helps customer service representatives understand how "good" customer service is defined and provides specific knowledge and decision rights to prevent giving customers what they want at all costs. Another example is a performance management sys-tem and approach that provides a clear understanding of what the company *actually* expects from their employees. Clear goals and objectives, assignment of responsibility to specific initiatives, and detailed timelines set expectations that not only help people man-age trade-offs inherent in their day-to-day work but also let others know who is responsible for what. We were surprised to learn that setting boundaries has absorbed a negative perception in many organizations – "consequences" equate to dissatisfaction, disci-pline, or penalty. To drive sustainable execution, organizational leaders need the courage and latitude to say "no" as well as enforce discipline, penalty, and termination when necessary. However, boundaries in everyday work can also be established in a more positive way. Regular reminders, constructive advice, and candor set a tone that someone is interested in the work people are doing and provide early warnings when people veer toward unproductive effort that causes resources to be wasted or exhausted.

Engagement Barrier

The final barrier preventing organizations from building capacity is disengagement of employees, customers, and other stakeholders, which results in lost productivity. In sustainable execution, engagement is not just a measure of how satisfied individuals are with their specific job, product, service or experience. Engagement highlights the commitment made by a collective group of stakeholders to achieve a set of goals and objectives. A 2011 landmark study by the Harris Poll found only 15 per cent of employees could articulate their company's goals and priorities,[14] because strategies and key performance metrics are formulated behind closed doors by a select group of people and the broader organization is not involved in the process. In sustainable execution, engagement barriers are less evident when goals and objectives are effectively socialized, validated, and valuated.

- *Socializing* goals does not suggest everyone be involved – this is often not feasible or productive – but it does suggest expanding involvement to include a broader scope of influence that can make a difference.
- *Validating* goals builds employees' confidence that they can achieve them. Stretch targets are good to set; however, unachievable goals do not foster engagement.
- *Valuating* the goals, with clear incentives, can help unleash discretionary effort. Financial incentives must always be

accompanied with public recognition of personal contributions to make them most meaningful and create a culture of high performance.

This inability to articulate goals and priorities is one of many challenges manifested in engagement barriers. Identifying a complete list of factors that deplete engagement is beyond the scope of this book; however, the crucial point is to recognize the impact of engagement barriers to execution. For example, lack of engagement causes customer service to deteriorate and targets and deadlines to be missed. There is also a waning discretionary effort from employees to dedicate extra time and energy to get the job done or volunteer to lead new initiatives. Lack of participation in both work (meetings) and non-work activities (e.g., charity drives and social events) is also a good indicator that engagement is a problem. Remember, people are more likely to double-down on their own interests over those of others.

Orchestrating the Capacity Shift

When organizations are effective at building capacity they not only grow revenue and profit, but they also grow alternative sources of energy such as capabilities, knowledge, and experience, making the organization more capable of sustaining growth over time. Through our research, we have uncovered three recommended approaches to building capacity.

Financial Trade-Offs

Capacity is heightened by stretching resources to increase productivity as well as supplying businesses that are ripe for growth and opportunity with the adequate resources they need. The assumption that what made your organization successful in the past will continue to drive success in the future can be fatal;[15] when change is on the horizon, making difficult trade-offs is essential for survival. In sustainable execution, organizations make trade-offs in several different ways.

Portfolio management forces business units to rethink ways they can maximize profitability from stable lines of business to feed higher growth opportunities in other business units. Its disciplined approach encourages budget planners to work together to identify areas of synergy and uncover opportunities to make an organization profitable. Table 3.1 illustrates a simple method for thinking about the role of portfolio management in building capacity in a "no-growth" scenario where revenue and cost of goods sold (COGS) are flat. To be profitable, a decrease in variable spending (i.e., labor, materials) is necessary to offset unavoidable increases in fixed spending (i.e., rent, insurance, supplies). However, once variable cost-saving opportunities are depleted (Year 3), organizations need to fundamentally rethink their business model to reduce fixed spending or COGS to remain profitable. Bold financial trade-offs encourage organizations to take risks that challenge the status quo. Resources may need to be pulled from stable, established cash "cows" (products or services that are "milked" for profit with minimum effort), and redirect them to opportunities or new "rising star" initiatives that require a higher ratio of resources in order to launch and grow them to a stable state.[16] When each product or service in a company's portfolio is examined this way, it becomes easy to compare them and find opportunities for resource reallocation to drive the greatest value.

Alternative budgeting methods such as zero-based budgeting (ZBB) and variable or flexible budgets[17] are used to test and validate how financial resources will be used to deliver on the organization's strategic goals and objectives. A study of 597 executives across North

Table 3.1 No-Growth Example

	Year 0	Year 1	Year 2	Year 3	Year 4	Year 5	5 Year % change
Revenue	1000	1000	1000	1000	1000	1000	0
COGS	600	600	600	600	600	600	0
Fixed spending	150	153	156	149	141	135	–10
Variable spending	150	141	132	132	132	131	–12
Profit	100	106	112	119	126	134	34

Growth: 1.00   Productivity: 6.59%
Inflation: 1.02
Earnings per share growth: 1.06

America conducted by Deloitte in 2014 concluded that 37 per cent of organizations failed to align their budget planning effectively with corporate strategy.[18] Similarly, 46 per cent of senior managers in our study felt their organization failed to invest sufficient effort in rethinking the budget for each new planning period. Alternative budgeting is an addition to a broad set of established lean management tools that help organizations reduce and eliminate resources caught in unproductive uses. A survey of 406 North American companies by Bain & Company found 38 per cent of organizations used ZBB in 2016, up from 10 per cent in 2014.[19] 3G Capital used ZBB when it merged H.J. Heinz with Kraft Foods in 2015, and the result was a 2.5-point price-to-earnings premium improvement over similar mergers.[20] Flexible budgets are an alternative approach to static budgets, which help organizations account for unanticipated changes in organizational or market activity. This best practice does not deem static budgets obsolete in sustainable execution; rather it speaks to the need for organizations to vary their budgeting approach to best suit the needs of the business. Experts encourage organizations to vary their budgeting approach by using static budgets to provide realistic goals and creating flexible budgets after each accounting period to illustrate how much is actually spent and earned.[21] To illustrate a real example, organizations rarely overlook the need to create a static budget to support a business case that justifies an expenditure or investment. Moving to flexible budgets encourages the organization to regularly demonstrate the return on actual dollars being spent in savings or other financial benefits achieved. Comparing the flexible budget against the static budget enables an ongoing budget practice that aims to ensure projects and initiatives with the most potential are allocated the talent and funding they need to succeed, and validate that projects are delivering the expected benefits.

Mergers, acquisitions, and outsourcing shift resources to leverage external skilled expertise, flexible staffing, increased efficiency, and risk reduction. Mergers and acquisitions make significant financial trade-offs to supply the organization with new products and services that expand their value proposition. Outsourcing shifts resources so the organization can focus energy on doing what they do best. When trade-offs are done right, organizations are able to go beyond what's expected by reducing waste and converting cumbersome business processes into flexible, co-produced, value-added services. Let's look at the example of Sotheby's, a British multinational corporation established in 1744 that is one of the world's largest brokers of fine and decorative art, jewelry, real estate, and collectibles. They underwent a significant shift in resources when they bought out eighty employees (5 per cent of its workforce) at an estimated $40 million at the end of 2015 and followed up with the acquisition of a twenty-two-month-old art advisory company, Art Agency, Partners (AAP) for $85 million in January 2016. This shift occurred following a steep decline in performance of Sotheby's shares, which had dropped 50 per cent since March 2015.[22] Ultimately, Sotheby's move to acquire AAP shifted resources to transform their business from a traditional, navel-gazing auction house to a client-first provider of art services. Capacity rose as AAP attracted an enviable client list in a very short

period of time by invoking a keen, creative, and adventurous cura-
torial eye as well as a fresh perspective on new market dynamics as
buyers entered from Asia, South America, and Eastern Europe. By
working to truly understand the needs and challenges of artists and
art customers, AAP is disrupting a once stable industry by innovating new services dedicated to estate and legacy planning for artists
and their heirs and new financial arrangements for customers making eight- and nine-figure transactions.[23]

Before engaging in a change to accounting practices and/or budget
planning approaches, we encourage organizations to be sensitive to
the fact that orchestrating financial trade-offs to build capacity in these
ways can be challenging. Some best practices require strong leadership capable of taking a frank look at past performance, anticipating
market projections, innovating new business models, and encouraging profit by technically "taking from Peter to pay Paul." If leadership is willing to recognize there is an issue, invest the time required
to redefine roles and responsibilities, and innovate budget processes,
the opportunity to build capacity is extreme. However, if leadership
is not yet on board – you might want to consider a different approach.

Digitalize Your Business

Companies leverage digital technology to build capacity by involving customers in their business processes and customizing services
to deliver what customers want at the right time. In many organizations, digital solutions are fundamentally changing business
as usual, and companies are taking risks that challenge the status
quo – the common term for this is "digitalizing your business." We
offer a few examples below.

- *Self-service kiosks* and *customer portals* provide customers greater
  opportunity for time savings and access to the information

they need to make decisions. McDonald's self-service ordering kiosks are a great example of customers taking on work in the value chain, which reduces costs associated with ordering and checkout. Organizations that have pursued this transformation approach are recognizing that investment in human resources is still necessary to not only monitor the customer experience and assist with machine problems or frustrations, but unleash new opportunities to help customers find what they need, answer any questions they may have, up-sell and cross-sell products and services, and offer a friendlier, helpful, personalized customer experience.

- *Digital marketing* builds capacity by promoting brands through various methods such as search engine optimization, data-driven and social media marketing, display advertising, etc. The Chili's restaurant chain spent millions to make food look good on social media, because they understand that today's customers want to experience the world visually,[24] and word-of-mouth marketing is a powerful asset. Customers share selfies with friends to share clothing and travel ideas, stream concerts to share live experiences, and Tweet about dining or retail encounters that have exceeded or failed to meet expectation. This is a great way to build capacity, as 92 per cent of customers believe suggestions from friends and family more than they do advertising.[25]
- *Analytics* extends automated self-service to provide customers with widespread access to services and data (knowledge), different options for performing their desired interaction, and the ability to customize their experience. Profitability in traditional banks is being eroded by small innovative startups (i.e., Fin-Techs) that are rethinking self-service to offer more holistic data-driven solutions that give customers what they genuinely want, find valuable, and are excited about.[26] Accenture estimates that the top twenty-five US banks are together overlooking $2 billion

in possible cost savings that will be taken by FinTechs if banks don't quickly change their mindset to driving value through data and analytics.

- *Digitally enabled partnerships* are essential in the digital age, as they can speed up the pace of change and create growth opportunities. McKinsey & Company Director Paul Willmott describes digital partnerships as "plug and play" dynamics that "stitch together" value offerings from different organizations to deliver fast solutions and services that satisfy customer needs and demands.[27] Take, for example, the partnership between New Zealand's large mobile app developer MEA Mobile that plugged their photo printing app (Printicular) into 8,000 Walgreens stores in the United States. Through limited investment, users can now edit and send photos directly from their phone and pick up pictures at their local Walgreens within an hour. Enabling this partnership, Walgreens Photo ranked amongst companies such as Shutterfly and Amazon Print as one of the best online photo-printing services in 2019.[28]

There is significant untapped potential using digital technology; however, designing solutions that actually build capacity is no easy task. Solutions need to infuse technology to promote cost savings and growth but also make sure real value is provided to customers in return for their effort. Any organization that has experienced a significant digitalization of their business understands that the dollars invested in technology are minimal compared to the investment made in managing change. As such, resourcing digital solutions as "corner of the desk"[29] initiatives is not recommended. In our experience, digital initiatives attract high levels of engagement as employees find them challenging and exciting, but digitalizing your business requires allocation of dedicated resources.

Modernize the Workplace

Employees who are asked to take risks and push performance beyond traditional limits require a modern workplace that orchestrates challenging goals, a healthy pressure to increase productivity, and day-to-day expression of value and recognition. Google is a classic example of a company that effectively strikes this balance. Topping Fortune's list as the "Best Company to Work For" year-over-year, the key to Google's success in building capacity is *intrinsic motivators* that extract outstanding ideas and high levels of productivity. Perks of working at Google range from free chef-prepared, organic food and haircuts, to subsidized massages and hybrid cars, to extended maternity benefits and takeout meal allowances for new parents. They empower their employees with added responsibility, recognize their accomplishments, and provide opportunities to pursue knowledge and learning to build confidence and esteem. Google is an example of an organization that recognizes that energy from talent is crucial for success. They justify expensive perks by recognizing costs associated with employee dissatisfaction and high turnover in their industry far exceed their investment in modernizing the workplace. They also recognize value is generated when people feel challenged in their work. Google understands people have enormous capacity for getting things done and place great value in recharging people with healthy food, exercise, and challenging goals.

Performance management is the science behind the modern work environment that is achieved by capturing and utilizing data to hire and retain extraordinary people and gauge employees to improve productivity. People deliver precisely what their compensation programs ask them to deliver, so compensation schemes need to stay aligned to the most current and relevant goals and objectives. Sixty per cent of organizations in our research agree their company fails to modify and adjust incentives and individual performance metrics to align to the annual operational goals and objectives. Goals and objectives change, but incentives remain the same. To build capacity, organizations also need to distribute ownership of performance management processes beyond the stronghold of human resource and finance departments, and provide the leadership team with the information necessary to communicate and own the incentives. When departments fail to take ownership, organizations experience peaks and valleys in performance – weeks where people achieve more than expected followed by weeks where it seems nothing gets done at all. All managers need to take responsibility for how their employees are rewarded and be accountable for establishing a daily rhythm that encourages people to deliver results day in and day out. A simple solution to establishing rhythm in highly transactional departments is a daily check-in – a short meeting at the same time each day where teams get together to review yesterday's progress and set a plan for today.

Finally, research from the University of Warwick Business School highlights the importance of *openness and transparency* in the modern workplace.[30] When people are motivated to share important news, either good or bad, a deeper level of clarity emerges that signals both strengths and potential weaknesses or challenges. Key to building capacity through openness and transparency is how the organization responds to indicators of under-performance such as a "red" on a corporate dashboard. A commitment to "celebrating the reds" changes a potentially negative situation into a positive response by drawing attention to an issue and providing an opportunity for proactive problem solving. Only 37 per cent of organizations in our research agree that a "red" on a corporate dashboard represents an opportunity to seek help; the majority see it as an admission of poor performance or failure. Celebrating the reds is achieved by establishing a policy where a "red" is a formal way of asking leadership for help. By doing so, leadership gains visibility into where their attention and action can help solve problems and, in turn, generate value. Following up with a routine that documents and shares lessons learned will prevent repeat occurrences of the same issues and challenges.

Although these approaches to orchestrating resources to build capacity grow revenues and create alternative sources of energy, they all require an investment that not all organizations are willing to make. Both digitalizing and modernizing the business attract high levels of engagement as employees find them challenging and exciting, but they require more financial support than just surplus. In fact, in most cases companies need to make a significant investment in overhauling legacy IT solutions and/or building modifications that many executives are unwilling to make. This brings us back to financial trade-offs and the importance of bold decisions and significant budget changes. It is easy to admire the behaviors of executives such as Ford's CEO Jim Hackett, but finding leaders willing to shift resources in this way is perhaps the biggest challenge in building capacity.

4

SHIFT ALIGNMENT TO
GENERATE MOMENTUM

"Alignment" is often the answer given when organizations are asked, "How do you execute your strategy?" The strategic planning regime aligns the organization to high-level goals and annual objectives by cascading objectives down the hierarchy, defining relevant metrics to measure progress, and providing the incentive for all employees to do their part. When it comes to execution, today's organizations understand that alignment through planning is not enough. Significant investment is made to establish a rhythmic approach to alignment through standardized processes, procedures, and policies that promote consistency and routine. Another popular alignment mechanism is key performance indicators (KPIs) that, when carefully managed, encourage the organization to drive results. Although most organizations can articulate how they establish alignment, executing in alignment is not easy. In fact, authors of *The Work of Leaders: How Vision, Alignment, and Execution Will Change the Way You Lead*, report that only 47 per cent of senior leaders have a clear understanding of what "building alignment" means in the context of leadership.[1] As a result, despite people working hard, they fail to deliver results.

Momentum in the sustainable execution model is generated when organizations orchestrate an execution system that enables steady and uniform day-to-day action to deliver on the organization's most important goals and objectives. Alignment generates momentum by directing time and effort toward a common set of goals in a manner that sustains energy, minimizes waste, and increases overall activity. Best practices such as total quality management (TQM), lean six sigma, and project management are extremely effective at generating momentum; however, too much standardization in these practices to drive efficiency and productivity can make it difficult to navigate a change in direction. The key to understanding this contraction is to recognize that inherent in momentum is inertia – a tendency to remain unchanged. As such, building alignment needs to go beyond strategic and operational planning that directs time and effort toward a common set of goals, to orchestrate day-to-day activity that optimizes efficiency and responds to change at the same time. The evolution in project management practice is a good example of modern thinking about alignment and momentum. For the most part, Agile and traditional projects have the same destination (i.e., goals and objectives) but prescribe distinctly different approaches for how goals will be achieved. Specifically,

- Traditional approaches plan, organize, and ideally freeze the scope of work to set clear expectations and define work across a long, interdependent sequence of activities. Any change to the plan requires adherence to a formal change procedure. Performance is monitored according to milestones, and when a variance in cost and/or schedule is detected, adjustments are made.
- Agile approaches execute work in smaller increments over a short period of time (i.e., sprints) to produce a useable product component. The sequence of tasks is executed multiple times, on faster timelines. Establishing an execution rhythm through shorter milestone cycles enables regular reviews and daily check-ins to make sure each small component aligns with the

previous one, as well as the overall goals and objectives for the project.

It is important to recognize that both methods are uniform in motion. Like traditional project processes, sprints and frameworks such as "scrums" establish a regular, repeatable work cycle that can generate momentum. It is the small increments that make the Agile approach better at adapting to changes in direction. In projects where change is necessary, generating momentum in this way makes sense. However, if the need for change is lower, traditional project approaches may generate more momentum and deliver superior results. This chapter explores how organizations can improve their backbone for execution by filling gaps that cause day-to-day activity to veer away from the company's most important goals and objectives.

What Is Momentum?

Momentum is the energy that sustains performance and increases productivity. Athletes on a trampoline require energy to get going, but once in motion their routine flows freely, as momentum fuels velocity and strengthens the stability of their performance. The effectiveness of the operational "whirlwind" of activity inside an organization thrives on similar energy. Momentum in an organization's energy system is evident when everyone has a consistent, coherent understanding of what the organization is trying to achieve, how work gets done, and why it matters. For leadership, generating momentum goes beyond delegating tasks, adhering to processes, and setting expectations for performance. It involves committing to thoughtful and ongoing conversations, careful monitoring to stay focused on delivering results, and offering insight when the organization is under-performing. As such, alignment requires organizations to create a dedicated practice regime similar to coaching a sport. Plans need to be driven from the top – coaches dedicate countless hours and leverage their expertise to create the plays, establish routines, and decide the assignment of roles and responsibilities. Each player is expected to contribute to and be able to recite the playbook. Practice is embedded in the planning regime, so teams are prepared when it comes time to execute. Players understand that good coaching creates value in the following ways:

- It evaluates the formal "playbook" of rules and processes to allow plans to be altered and course corrections to be made.
- It encourages informal routines and common vocabulary to emerge that enables team building, communication. and coordination.
- It establishes a clear understanding of how decisions will be made to avoid conflict and confusion.

In organizations, generating momentum starts with setting clear expectations about what the company is trying to achieve, the tactics that will achieve the objectives, and the metrics that will be used to measure performance. As there are endless possibilities how an organization will succeed, sustainable execution takes guidance from the 80/20 rule, or the law of the **vital few**. In each year the late Steve Jobs pushed his top 100 executives to identify the ten leading objectives in an off-site planning retreat – near the end, he took a marker and crossed out the bottom seven. "We can only do three," he would announce. Shifting the executive's focus clearly differentiated the top goals from those less important and aligned resources to a set of realistic and achievable goals for the organization. As illustrated in figure 4.1, an *achievable set of goals and objectives* establish the target for consistent and routine behavior so momentum can build and the rate of activity can increase. To execute well, organizations need to

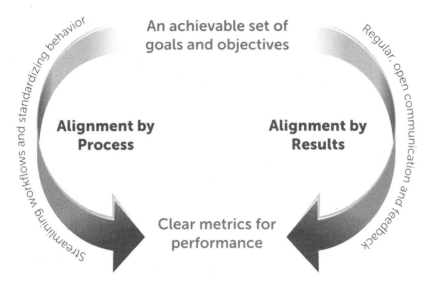

Figure 4.1 Sustainable Execution Approach to Shift Alignment

be steadfast in keeping time and energy aligned to achieving these goals. If work deviates from the target, energy will be lost.

Generating momentum also requires that organizations set and communicate *clear metrics for performance* that not only empower people to take action but enable the business to gain momentum from past successes. Take, for example, a sports team that goes on a winning streak, players, and coaches react to consecutive wins by innovating plays and working harder to increase their odds of winning again. In organizations, measuring and reporting progress on dashboards and burn charts[2] encourage people to maintain effort and work hard. Modern execution approaches that execute in smaller increments experience the benefits of gaining momentum, as regular "wins" enable a streak of performance energized by celebrating and rewarding past success.

In sustainable execution, two additional capabilities establish alternative ways an organization can shift an execution system into alignment and generate momentum. The first is a disciplined, systematic capability that establishes consistency and routine by organizing day-to-day activity through an intense focus on process improvement and problem solving.[3] *Alignment by process* generates momentum of day-to-day activity by streamlining workflows and standardizing behavior to increase the rate of activity. In this approach, people are held accountable to following procedure by performance metrics that measure the degree to which day-to-day activity is following the established protocol. This approach can be extremely effective in aligning daily work to quality targets, as well as establishing consistency in the customer experience. Execution systems such as Lean Six Sigma provide organizations with guidance and data-driven tools and methodologies for choosing what needs to be done, monitoring performance, solving problems, and delivering quantifiable results. Top companies such as General Electric, AlliedSignal, and Motorola have generated momentum by using this approach and maximized efficiency and productivity as a result.[4]

The alternative capability recognizes that organizations require more than a bundle of processes or boxes on an organizational chart to hold people accountable.[5] Momentum increases through *alignment by results* when people are empowered to deliver results, and performance metrics measure outcomes that give people more latitude and autonomy in determining how they will do the work. This approach to alignment is encouraged where formalized processes feel unnecessary or burdensome and authority is more decentralized. In our experience, companies that do this well implement strong reinforcement activities (e.g., town halls, visual models, all-employee update calls, etc.) that allow for clarification and guidance through two-way communication. Globally disbursed organizations, universities, and professional services firms are good examples of how flexible approaches to work and autonomy drive day-to-day activity such that alignment is only as strong as its weakest link.[6] In these industries, one voice or one small group out of alignment can make the difference between success and failure. *Alignment by results* generates momentum of day-to-day activity through regular, open communication and feedback to keep people aligned and increase the rate of activity. It makes day-to-day activity more nimble and flexible, as new information is regularly shared and discussed so the path forward can be adjusted.

There a few final points to be made about figure 4.1 before we move on. First, execution systems that leverage both process and results in tandem generate unprecedented momentum for getting things done. Alignment by process communicates and coordinates work in routine and simple ways, to the point where adjustments in behavior can be inspired by a simple look or gesture. Alignment by results encourages people to make exceptions and modifications to process to accommodate a change in market activity or customer demand. This is a great example of how organizations will benefit by abandoning the underlying *choisir une voie* mentality that suggests execution practice needs to "pick a lane" between practices that drive results through stability and those that promote flexibility. Next, many organizations spend weeks, if not months, crafting the strategy and get stumped when we ask them how much time they've set aside to execute it. Planning hours invested in identifying an achievable set of common goals, determining the right balance between process and results, and establishing appropriate and clear metrics to motivate behavior are significant. Even after the investment in planning, more time in meetings and town halls is essential to examine employee reactions and generate input and feedback necessary for evaluating trade-offs and making appropriate adjustments. So how long does this take? In large organizations, this could take months, making the strategy obsolete by the time the organization is ready to execute. As such, identifying barriers and orchestrating best practices are important to generating momentum in ways that align the organization to the most important goals and objectives without decreasing the rate of activity.

Barriers to Generating Momentum

Figure 4.2 uses a wind turbine analogy to illustrate how potential barriers to structure (alignment), rhythm (consistency), and aware- ness (objectivity) must be orchestrated to generate momentum and maximize output. Essential to the organization's energy system, the turbine generates momentum by keeping day-to-day action aligned to deliver on strategic goals and objectives. When barriers arise the result is as if the blades are broken off. The turbine goes out of align- ment, energy is lost, and optimum output cannot be realized. Orga- nizations need to fill gaps to repair the broken blades that impede momentum and break down the execution system.

At a high level, the three barriers to momentum prevent people from knowing "what" they need to do, "how" to do it, and "why" it matters. A simple example is the case of the *burnt bagel*. A customer orders a bagel toasted with butter and a coffee, at a popular drive- thru coffee house. After paying for the order, she swiftly exits the fast- moving drive-thru lineup with bagel and coffee in hand. It is not until she has settled into her daily commute that she unwraps the bagel and realizes it is burned – not just slightly, but burned black. When she took her complaint to social media, she learned that this was not an isolated incident – others had experienced that same problem. *Why* would an employee at the popular coffee house butter a scorched bagel, wrap it in wax paper, and deliver it the customer? Clearly poor product quality is not part of the coffee house's strategy; something else must have influenced the employee's behavior. No matter the reason, this simple example raises a very relevant question. Why do

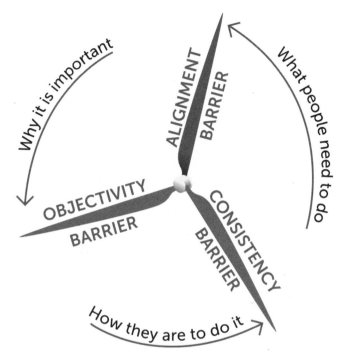

Figure 4.2 Barriers to Generating Momentum

companies with sound strategies repeatedly disappoint their custom-ers? Shifting the organization into alignment is important, because repeated "burnt bagel" customer experiences will eventually deplete opportunities for growth and performance. In a very real way, the momentum behind what people do and how they behave defines the customer experience. Linking this example to sustainable execu-tion shows that shifting alignment is essential, as *execution is the only strategy the customer sees*. So if frontline employees are getting things wrong in your organization, it may be because there are gaps in their understanding of what they need to do, how they do it, and/or why it matters.

Alignment Barrier

Simply stated, people prioritize and perform work on the basis of their understanding of the goals and objectives, what incentives are being used, and whether or not people are responsible and accountable. When any of these are unclear or misaligned, day-to-day behavior fails to deliver on the strategy. Structuring alignment between goals, objectives, tactics, and metrics, and assigning clear accountability may seem like a basic approach used in planning; however, our research uncovered some surprising results:

- Eighty per cent of managers agree that their organization *pursues too many goals and objectives* at same time. When strategy cascades down the organization, business units need a way to align their annual goals to the overall strategic direction. Without an alignment mechanism to do that, departments pursue too many goals, or their own goals are based on what they feel is important.
- An overwhelming 78 per cent of organizations agree their organization needs to conduct *more detailed planning of operational activities*. This view may sound surprising, as the majority of organizations create annual operating plans; however, in our experience the level of detail is limited to describing how money will be spent and the tactics involved. Good operating plans go further to make trade-offs in where people need to focus time and resources, how work will be aligned (i.e., updated work-flows, communication plans), and clear indication of metrics that explain why the work is important.
- Even though the majority of organizations had adopted balanced scorecard[7] or other best practices for using metrics to drive execution, 57 per cent of organizations agreed their organization was *reporting on the wrong metrics*. Performance metrics were

tracking and measuring many things, but the portfolio of metrics fell short in driving performance.

Alignment barriers also arise when the elements of the strategy (i.e., objectives, tactics, processes, and incentives) fail to be simplified and communicated in a way that aligns it to the day-to-day whirlwind of activity. Operational planning becomes so focused on tasks and "to do" list that people lose the sense of purpose behind their work that inspires productivity and achieves results. Organizations that get the best performance out of their people generate momentum by linking goals and objectives to day-to-day work. One executive explained how once a week he walked around and asked people what they were working on. After they responded, he asked a second question: "How does that align to our top goals?" He went on to clarify that he was not really looking for an answer, he just wanted people to make the connection.

Consistency Barrier

Consistency is a form of rhythm that places execution in "a groove" by establishing a pattern for performance that heightens productivity and confidence. No matter how much investment is made in planning for alignment, the whirlwind of daily activity will veer off course. Consistency fuels the momentum they need to recover and get back on track. Returning to the trampolinist analogy, consistency allows for an off-center jump to be corrected in the air so the athlete can get performance back into "the zone" on the very next bounce. Similarly, when planned activity in organizations gets derailed by a setback, consistency helps teams recover "on the fly" and maintain productivity.

Barriers to consistency arise when organizations fail to *establish discipline through standardized work*. The journey to consistent and predictable results is arduous, so establishing clear work routines where appropriate minimizes waste. People waste less time piecing together fragmented processes and generate confidence in their work so they can take charge of responsibilities and make sound judgments when required.

Our research found that even some organizations that heavily invest in standardized work continue to struggle with execution in times of adversity. Specifically, people lack resilience when faced with risk. Organizations that avoid this barrier put their plans and standard procedures through a *rigorous regime of practice* to articulate when standardized work is problematic and how the business needs to make exceptions. Sports teams and military units illustrate how generating consistency through practice can dramatically improve an organization's ability to execute. Modern methods such as Kata[8] and Agile provide companies with ways to create safe and low-cost practice approaches that help generate feedback and prepare employees to be more resilient. Kata is a lean Six-Sigma management approach developed by Toyota that establishes a practice for continuous improvement through the scientific problem-solving method of "Plan, Do, Check, Act," as well as a coaching practice that helps executives challenge their assumptions and change the way they think and act. Companies such as Bell Canada have adopted Kata to execute high-risk business processes such as network security and manufacturing, and the health-care industry is using it to plan and anticipate problems that save lives.[9] The Agile methodology encourages practice by iterating through small batches of work (or sprints) and promoting the concept of "fail forward," so results from poor execution are identified when changes are less costly to make. Failing forward gives the team feedback at a time when leadership can react positively as opposed to later in the project when the stakes are higher and leadership has less tolerance and patience. Through practice, Agile approaches work out the "kinks" early and establish routines that drive results.

Finally, consistency barriers arise when organizations *use words and acronyms* (i.e., *vocabulary*) that are ill-defined, unknown, or ambiguous. Think back to your last discussion with finance and/or information technology (IT) and count the number of unfamiliar acronyms and terms they assumed you understood. Vague (e.g., leadership, culture) and topical words (e.g., Big Data, Agile, Digital) are especially problematic when they are used to set direction. We have come across several catch phrases that we encourage organizations to use with extreme caution:

- "Our approach to driving results is to improve our culture."
- "To execute well we need stronger leadership."
- "The key to giving our customers what they want is to go digital."
- "Big data and analytics are core to our company's strategy."
- "We can save the organization money but putting IT in the cloud."
- "Our plan for the coming year is to become more agile."

To illustrate the power of consistent vocabulary, we share a story about a large bank that was having a problem with their data scientists using statistical terms and knowledge to overpower business analysts and interpreting results in inappropriate or irrelevant ways. To address this problem, we helped the organization create "dance styles" that prescribed a specific code of conduct for who would "lead" each analytics project. Each dance style brought with it a different set of expectations and procedures. For example, if the leadership defined a project as a "tango," that meant they wanted the generation of insights to be led by the data scientist, as the "truth" was expected to be counterintuitive to the intuition of the business. A project assigned as a "waltz" set the expectation for a shared insight approach, as it wasn't clear whether the "truth" was in the data or the experience of the business, so the two analysts needed to work closely together. Leveraging the power of common vocabulary, the bank quickly realized consistency promotes benefits similar to standardization but in a much more flexible way.

Objectivity Barrier

The final barrier in this shift is lack of objectivity, which is an awareness barrier that can be caused by an organization's decision-making. If decisions are not given due process and/or the process lacks transparency, people may not understand how decisions are made. *Being transparent* is good practice but more essential when decisions are likely to create dissent. Walking people through the process helps them understand and respect decisions. Research shows that twenty-first-century employees have higher expectations of employers being open and transparent about the decisions they make – specifically when deciding on sensitive or controversial issues. When leaders make decisions that are perceived unjust, tomorrow's up-and-comers will not think twice about looking for another job.[10]

When moving through a business process that requires approvals, momentum is often lost as people stand idle waiting for approvals. Although many organizations have formalized processes for making decisions, only 32 per cent have a *formal process for prioritizing decisions.* Without clear priority, people are sidetracked and waste time on decisions that matter less. Another factor is that without clear priority, hard decisions are often treated as the elephant in the room. Everybody knows it is there, but no one wants to address it. As a result, secondary decisions naturally take priority, and delaying the difficult decisions ends up creating bigger problems.

Finally, objectivity barriers arise when decision-making is *biased or politically charged.* Today's organizations are becoming less tolerant of inappropriate use of power and politics in decision-making. Objectivity demands that organizations seek and value awareness and take action to ensure the "right" decisions are made (e.g., the "right" projects get funded, the "best" people get promoted), and those with a need to know are informed. Relevant decisions need to be appropriately socialized by giving employees a safe place to speak their mind (e.g., meeting, online discussion forum, email thread), to seek opinion, and most importantly, to generate a sincere level of "buy-in." Key to understanding how to address this source of objectivity is to define *appropriate*. First, inviting people to be frank about decisions that are beyond their pay grade can muddy the waters about who is actually in charge. Decision rights come with accountability, and only those willing to be accountable should be empowered to influence decisions. Second, silence needs to mean agreement, because once a decision is made, people need to hold their tongue. This prevents any backlash from those who had the opportunity to be frank, open, and honest but chose not to be.

Orchestrating the Alignment Shift

Now that we have described the major barriers that need to be considered to manage a shift in alignment, let's look at several approaches that may be helpful in facilitating a shift to overcome these barriers.

Goal Setting

The process of goal setting articulates the strategy so all employees can understand what needs to be done and where they fit in. It is a planning approach that gets everyone on the same page so people plan work that aligns to the organization's most important objectives. There are four steps to the process and each has many

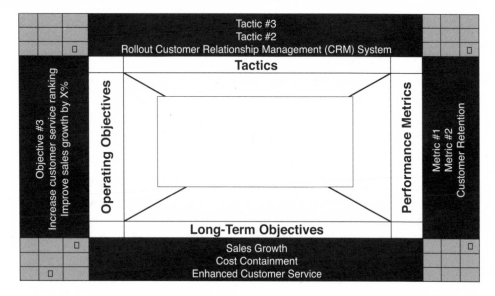

Figure 4.3 Hoshin Corporate X-Matrix

alternative exercises and templates that can be used. We offer a few below.

Step #1: Connect individual goals to the organizational mandate. Figure 4.3 illustrates a tool from the Hoshin Kanri regime[11] that is used by companies such as 3M, Nike, and HP Inc. In sustainable execution, we recommend the X-matrix be used to develop comprehensive goals. All too often goal setting is vague and motivated by the need to define compensation and bonus plans. This tool helps organizations connect individual goals (i.e., objectives, tactics) that drive motivation to the higher-level organizational mandate (i.e., long-term objectives) and results (i.e., metrics). The one-page map creates a visual representation so people can easily understand how their objectives and tactics (e.g., roll out customer relationship management [CRM] system) align to what the organization is trying to achieve (e.g.,

sales growth, cost containment, and *customer service*) and the performance metrics (e.g., customer retention) they will affect. The
four corners of the X-matrix enable careful alignment between
individual and organizational goals; specifically, the location of
the X defines the connection. For example, the X in the top right
and bottom right corners indicate the CRM rollout will be implemented to increase customer retention to achieve sales growth.
Mapping the goal in this ways makes it clear the project manager will pursue the CRM rollout in a way that retains customers
who drive growth – or perhaps release customers who do not.
If the X in the bottom corner was moved to connect *retention* to
customer service, the overall goal of the CRM rollout would be to
enhance service for all customers. Although the distinction may
seem simple, enhancing alignment in this way has helped many
organizations narrow the gap between intention (the plan) and
implementation (the work). Clarifying how performance will
be measured up front (i.e., retention to drive sales growth) is
extremely helpful in connecting individual goals to the higher-
level organizational mandate.

Step #2: Socialize the goals. Once goals are in place, an investment needs to be made in socializing the goals, obtaining feedback,
and gaining support. Catch ball[12] is a socialization method that conducts a series of team meetings across management levels to clarify
goals and make adjustments. Objectivity is also enhanced as collective decisions are made openly and transparently. Playing catch ball
requires effort; however, with practice the process becomes more
efficient.

Step #3: Align goals across the organization. The practice of
aligning goals encourages organizations to recognize that when
operational planning and budgets cascade down the organization,
clear goals and accountability need to follow. By cascading CEO-
level goals down the organization to influence second-level (VP)

Table 4.1 Cascading Goals

CEO level: $Y = f(x_1, x_2, x_3 ...)$	
Y = Grow a specific product line.	x_1: Increase sales revenue (sales)
	x_2: **Launch product-marketing campaigns (marketing)**
	x_3: Hire sales representatives and update training (HR)
	x_4: Revise sales incentive plan (HR)
VP level: Marketing $Y = f(x_1, x_2, x_3 ...)$	
Y = Launch product-marketing campaigns.	x_1: Hire marketing analysts.
	x_2: **Launch customer focus-group initiative.**
	x_3: Develop and launch a customer insight web portal.
Director level: $Y = f(x_1, x_2, x_3 ...)$	
Y = Launch customer focus-group initiative.	x_1: Design focus groups to represent the customer base.
	x_2: Complete 25 focus groups across the country.
	x_3: Analyze and report customer insights.

and third-level (director) goals, inherently everyone starts moving in the same direction. Table 4.1 illustrates a Six Sigma tool that uses the simple mathematical term $Y = f(x)$ to articulate the fact that high-level strategic goals (Ys) are achieved by lower-level operational goals (xs).

In this example, a CEO-level goal to grow a specific product line (Y) cascades to four lower-level goals (xs) that distribute accountability among Sales, Marketing, and HR for achieving that goal. At the VP level, their higher-level goals (Ys) align to director-level goals (xs) that influence goal setting and accountability of specific work teams. As the Ys and xs cascade down the organization, it becomes clear how goals will be achieved and who is accountable. Using this approach, if growth targets are not being achieved, the CEO knows exactly who to talk to uncover the source of the problem. It might be because Sales is not driving revenue or Marketing did not hire enough marketing analysts, or it could be that the CEO failed to identify an objective or tactic (e.g., technology innovation) essential to achieving the growth agenda.

Operational Excellence

Operational excellence is a continuation of goal setting that extends alignment to day-to-day activity and keeps everyone on the same page by doing work that delivers on the organization's most important objectives. Again, there are many alternative exercises and templates that can be used, and we offer a few of our favorites below.

- **Careful metrics design.** "You can't manage what you don't measure" is certainly relevant when it comes to operational excellence; however, a careful approach to metrics design is essential to make sure the use of metrics is driving the desired day-to-day behavior. First, using too many metrics creates confusion and reduces momentum, so good design practice is to remove a metric at the same time one is added. Next, keep the two alignment paths (figure 4.1) when designing metrics. Process metrics (e.g., number of sales leads, number of investor plans completed) are effective at streamlining workflows and standardizing behavior to increase the rate of activity, and results metrics (e.g., new sales dollars) are effective when people need more latitude and autonomy in how they will do the work.
- A **storyboard** that describes what and when specific tactics will be implemented. Storyboards are more effective than traditional timelines and Gantt charts, as they communicate a success story made up of problems that need solutions. In stories, outcomes are used to articulate what each tactic will yield, as opposed to what will be done. This slight modification to describing tactics makes the tactics more relevant to the organization.
- **Status reports** that draw attention to issues, problems, or risks that interfere with getting the work done. Calling attention to too many issues undermines operational excellence, as it draws unnecessary attention to issues that are premature. Important

issues are the most debilitating, yet feasible. Nothing is more frustrating for leadership than a list of issues they cannot do anything about (e.g., market dynamics, policy, regulatory standards, etc.). Perhaps most important are issues that are urgent, making the timeliness of status reports important. Periodic status reports are effective at establishing consistency, but there also needs to be a way (e.g., five-minute daily stand-up meeting) people can call attention to urgent issues that require immediate attention.

- Finally, a clear assignment of who is **responsible and accountable** for tasks and issues. Incorporating a tool such as a RACI Responsibility Matrix[13] establishes a cadence of accountability to operations that is essential to execution.

"Smart" Workflow Optimization

We found the most common approach to generating momentum in organizations is standardizing and optimizing work. Organizations are not only turning to business process management (BPM)[14] to drive efficiency and cost reduction, they are also using process models and engaging process owners to drive change when there is no time to put a complete change program in place. When processes are standardized, the organization is more certain about achieving a consistent output, and internal auditors and/or outside regulatory bodies are more likely to be satisfied. Other benefits of reducing variability include reduction in time and costs to train and transition people between jobs, reduced injuries and stress, and enables continuous improvement.

Through our research, we found organizations tended to invest in workflow optimization for complex business processes but overlooked its benefits for simpler tasks. For example, we worked with one organization to establish a process for prioritizing decisions, as they were struggling with an objectivity barrier that was causing people to stand idle, waiting for approvals. Together we created the following process:

- *Set aside a specific time each week (or each day)* to review approval requests. This was important because some people were very effective at getting the answers they needed. Tactics such as stalking leadership in hallways, derailing other meeting agendas, or marking their emails as urgent enabled opportunistic behavior.
- *Flag emails* requesting approval. Sometimes delays are caused simply by a communication issue. The company institutionalized a way to flag and prioritize emails that required action to expedite decision making.
- Implement a *"deferral" status* to indicate when a decision has been deferred because more time to review the request is needed. Putting decisions formally "on hold" with a clear plan of action helped people mitigate risks that evolved from the delay.
- Formalize a way to *hold leadership accountable* for making difficult decisions (e.g., employee termination, demotion, dealing with workplace conflict) that are stalling progress. This one was not easy – they experimented with anonymous employee feedback systems and a whistleblowing policy but decided on a structured issue resolution process that guided employees and managers in resolving workplace issues and clearly indicated points where leadership was required to get involved.

Finally, the trend toward "smart" workflows enabled by digital technology propels the benefits of consistency to an entirely new level. The last few decades have reaped the benefits of automation – service reliability, cost reduction, and reduced human error, to name a few. Today, innovations in artificial intelligence and Internet of

Things (IoT) are making automated workflows "smart" – capable of distributing real-time information, making decisions, learning, and adapting to changes in the outside environment. When it comes to execution, the benefits of "smart" workflow optimization are clear.

PART THREE

Removing Distractions

This discussion marks the half-way-point in our Shift-to-Execute framework (table 2.3). At this point we pivot away from *increasing energy by filling gaps* to describe ways organizations can *conserve energy by removing distractions* across the organization. Removing distractions allows energy to be shared through synergy and minimizes the diversion and loss of energy through focus. Sharing and preventing energy loss are as important as creating it when it comes to lowering the cost of execution.

At this point, the wind turbine analogy expands to a wind farm, as the scope of sustainable execution moves beyond filling gaps in the execution backbone to removing distractions that interfere with how people and business units (i.e., multiple turbines) work together to deliver results. When turbines are too far part, energy cannot be shared, and valuable energy is lost. The right data are not available to the right people at the right time, and overbearing control slows down progress. Energy is wasted on lower-priority initiatives and unprofitable lines of business. Finally, cultural issues arise as departments or groups do not share information or as they get trapped in their own experience. It is these next two chapters that accelerate organizations toward more sustainable, economically viable execution systems. Each chapter explains the related barriers as well as specific ways organizations can orchestrate structure, rhythm, and awareness to complete the pathway for improvement.

5

SHIFT COLLABORATION TO PROMOTE SYNERGY

One of the most fundamental challenges facing today's leaders is keeping up in a rapidly changing world. Today's organizations are eager to trade in their traditional "plan, monitor, and adjust" regimes for more nimble, incremental management approaches that promote speed and agility. However, obstructing the path to driving results in modern ways are traditional top-down hierarchy and organizational silos.[1] When responsibilities and resources are assigned to departments across silos on the organization chart, even the most powerful incentives to work together are not enough. In fact, our research found that 64 per cent of organizations agreed that being too focused on the demands of their department or business unit plagued their desire and ability to collaborate and work together across functions. Take, for example, the inherent disconnect between revenue drivers (i.e., sales, marketing) and departments deemed administrative or support (e.g., HR, quality, IT). Efforts to change a human resource policy or implement a new quality assurance program are marginalized or overshadowed by initiatives that drive sales or increase profit. Another example is business and IT – for many reasons, the relationship between silos is strained, such as when IT policies and procedures slow down the business rather than speed it up.

Since the early 1990s, organizations have been re-engineering workflows and business processes to improve how work is done across traditional organizational silos. Supply chain management and CRM initiatives are examples of how integrated, cross-functional systems can transform work in an effort to reduce costs, integrate services, and personalize offerings for customers. Research completed by the Boston Consulting Group found that since 1997, cross-functional processes in US and European companies have increased anywhere from 50 to 350 per cent.[2] Success stories such as Walmart and Zara have relied on integrated systems for scaling up and improving efficiency. In sustainable execution, rethinking work and re-engineering processes is fundamental to generating momentum through alignment; however, through our research we learned that filling gaps does not necessarily enable collaboration. In fact, our research found 68 per cent of organizations that had invested in enterprise-wide technology solutions (e.g., Enterprise Resource Planning [ERP], CRM) disagreed that their employees had easy and timely access to information they needed to do their jobs. A study by McKinsey[3] found a similar result as interaction workers (those who interact with other people often, such as managers and salespeople) spend about 28 per cent of the workweek managing email and nearly 20 per cent looking for internal information to complete certain tasks.

Let's consider an example of an organization aspiring to get their Sales and Customer Service departments to work together more closely. Co-locating the two departments, implementing a cross-functional system, and establishing joint incentives are not enough. To promote collaboration, barriers to information flow and departmental culture also need to be addressed. Unfortunately, many leaders like to assume alignment equals collaboration, but highly processed organizations can actually create distractions that make true collaboration difficult. A sturdy execution backbone (e.g., hierarchy, process, and approvals) can have stifling effects on great ideas, initiatives, or projects that if left unaddressed can be fatal. It can also force people to "go around the system" to get things done. A common indicator of a collaboration problem is the endless hours spent in meetings to coordinate work across existing processes and navigate decision authority and competing objectives across silos. As today's organizations aspire for speed and agility, removing distractions from too many meetings is a great example of why this shift is essential for success. Let's consider a few other culprits that get in the way of people working effectively together.

- Shared goals are defined but the potential benefit is more significant for some stakeholders than others.
- Organizations mandate the use of collaboration tools that are not aligned to day-to-day work, so using them is more of a distraction than a benefit.
- Initiatives span business functions or silos that have contrasting opinions or views, making it difficult to share information and manage expectations.
- Everyone receives the same reward for performance, so some (i.e., non-contributors) take advantage and ride the coattails of others, giving little in return.
- People are unwilling to expand their role and/or responsibility, stagnating work they deem "not their job."
- Sub-organizations with different cultures and distinct organizational routines (e.g., merger, acquisition) are permitted to operate independently.

What Is Synergy?

In sustainable execution, synergy is a state of execution that occurs when alignment and collaboration come together to achieve results greater than the sum of their parts (i.e., $1 + 1 = 3$). When organizations experience synergy, there is a certain hum or state of activity where people are committed and aligned to a common purpose, information is seamlessly shared, and decisions are made that satisfy the competing demands of stakeholders in the most optimal way. The goal is to get alignment and collaboration to work in tandem. Going back to the IT example, co-locating them with the business and adjusting incentives may fill the gaps, but removing distractions to heighten the day-to-day interaction between departments requires an entirely different approach to execution. Unfortunately, the latter is too often marginalized, and organizations quickly learn that alignment is necessary for synergy but not sufficient.

Shifting collaboration to promote synergy orchestrates an energy system where organizations are highly committed to knowing what is going on across silos in their own organization as well as externally with partners, customers, and even competitors. In a state of synergy, leaders are willing to roll up their sleeves to identify and remove distractions that prevent people and work coming together. For example, we've come across a number of organizations where the key to resolving a barrier between two departments is a difficult conversation facilitated by the senior management team. Admittedly, some leaders find the need to facilitate difficult conversations frustrating; they prefer to "empower" departments to figure it out on their own. Sometimes this works, but sometimes it does not. To create synergy, leaders must be aware that there is a problem and make a conscious choice when to intervene and when to leave it alone.

Whether organizations aspire for synergy across silos or with an external network of partners, we've found the ability to share energy through collaboration is so powerful that it can accelerate execution to the point of defeating the odds. For example, companies such as Facebook promote synergy through a "workathon" approach to execution.[4] Specifically, they host a specific type of workathon called a "hackathon" to bring people together for two or three days to create a technology solution. The "Like" button and "Timeline" both evolved from these highly collaborative events. GroupMe (a mobile group messaging app acquired by Skype for $68 million) and Easy-Taxi (most downloaded taxi app in the world) were also the result of hackathons conceived at industry conferences such as TechCrunch and Startup Weekend.

So how can organizations share energy through collaboration? Our research uncovered a sustainable execution approach we illustrate using our wind farm analogy (figure 5.1) to show how multiple turbines (e.g., departments, organizations) can work in close proximity to each other through three capabilities that emulate how people communicate and connect.

Data streams represent the *capability to get the right information to the right people at the right time.* Many organizations turn to technology to enable data streams. They adopt tools such as Slack, LeanKit, Trello, and WhatsApp in an effort to provide real-time communication benefits where teams can easily message one another, store and archive messages, and streamline and manage tasks and workflows. An employee waiting on an approval needs efficient, real-time access to information, as do customers wanting to know if their product has shipped and when it will arrive. Data streams can also promote information sharing to bring people, data, and ideas together to encourage innovation. Co-locating a workathon team in a room for two or three days allows natural data streams to emerge. Online initiatives such as My Starbucks Idea[5] inspired a data stream that delivered more than

Figure 5.1 Sustainable Execution Approach to Shift Collaboration

190,000 ideas and over 300 new products and services, including Cake Pops, hazelnut macchiato, and free in-store Wi-Fi.

Insight valleys represent the *capability to heighten transparency and commitment to address issues and solve problems.* Synergy can be achieved only if people feel that their voice matters and others have their back. When organizations lack transparency, or their commitment to customers, partners, and employees comes into question, confidence and trust break down. On the other hand, high-trust environments inspire communication, as people don't second guess one another and are willing to go the extra mile to ensure that goals are met. When organizational leaders do a "deep dive" to explore what is really going on, they enter a valley where deep-rooted insights emerge that explain the root cause behind issues and problems. By removing these distractions, behavior tends to naturally evolve into making decisions and choices that are right, best, and highly valued by everyone involved.

Finally, **novelty hills** represent the *capability to achieve a common purpose by working across departments and business units to create something greater than the sum of parts.* In every collaborative initiative, there are a group of departments (i.e., hills) equipped to contribute, and inherently every department is most interested in what they have to offer. Novelty is the idea that although every department has something unique to offer, their skills and contributions are not necessarily the same. Empowering one department to be accountable and take charge may be essential to achieving their common purpose. When other departments refuse to follow another lead, they create a distraction that consumes valuable energy. Novelty also highlights the need to share leadership across departments; always allowing the same department to take the lead and repeatedly denying others is another common distraction. Finally, synergy is lost when strong performers (i.e., individuals, departments) are continuously required to compensate for weaker performers, impeding collaboration from reaching its fullest potential.

Barriers to Promoting Synergy

Barriers to promoting synergy are inherent in the degree to which factors such as busyness, competition for resources, and the uncertainty of changing market forces distract people from collaborating and working together. Even though organizations see value in synergy and aspire to be more collaborative, growing demands on employees and trends toward virtual work make it increasingly difficult to find time and opportunity to collaborate. Taking action on poor performance is also challenging in today's environment, as employee rights are top-of-mind and leadership have to practice caution to make sure their actions are justified. Finally, true collaboration requires that people assign importance to the common purpose more than to their own individual needs or wants. The three collaboration barriers in our sustainable execution model expand on these common distractions.

Integration Barrier

The first barrier highlights a common condition that arises when organizations encourage collaboration but fail to invest sufficient time and energy to identify the desired endgame and provide the right tools for integration. These barriers are very common when major changes to collaboration take place (i.e., mergers or acquisitions) but also arise from smaller changes such as investments in technology and data analytics to streamline work across departments. New systems and excessive data can actually create distractions that prevent organizations from driving benefits. A business ailment commonly referred to as "data rich, information poor" (DRIP) is a good example; one area of the business focused on investing in mountains of data actually creates a distraction for other business units trying to convert data into useful information. The result is slow "drips" of insight that actually generate value for the business. When the endgame for integration and preferred toolsets are not clearly defined and agreed upon, the result is two entities wasting energy as they pull in different directions. Imagine two chefs collaborating to make one dish from two different recipes and ingredient lists. As a result, investments in collaboration are seen as unnecessary collective efforts that eventually lead to diminishing returns.[6]

To describe the set of distractions that cause an integration barrier to arise, we share a story about an organization that had implemented a new CRM tool to enable collaboration with customers as well as the internal Sales and Support teams. They had strong executive buy-in and trained everyone to use the tool, but there was still limited uptake in changing the way people collaborated and worked together. People recognized the value in more data and information but did not really understand how they could use the data to encourage collaboration and drive value. The company created an inter-departmental task force and gave them one month to explore novel ways they could use the data and information. After one week, specific cases and value propositions started to emerge. They realized the following issues:

- Standardizing the use of the system was challenging, as users generated benefit in different ways. Some extracted value from using data and information to inform day-to-day operations, while others depended on data to run analysis on potential new product and service opportunities. The distraction was that people *didn't really understand how to leverage new data and information to inspire collaboration and better do their job.* Once standardized uses were identified and shared, people started to understand the potential value related to their specific job, and benefits from collaboration started to emerge.
- People found the *need to access an entirely new system* distracting. As such, the company explored ways they could embed CRM functionality into existing technology platforms and workflows. We encourage all leaders involved in making technology investment decisions to note that no collaboration tool should be confined to its own proprietary interface or departmental

silo. People have little to no appetite for using anything new, so collaborative tools need to be simple and seamlessly integrated with existing technology and workflows.

- Finally, the task force realized the company had invested in *functionality they really didn't need*, and training users on the entire suite of functionality made it difficult to determine what was really valuable. To quote the CIO, "It took us a while to truly understand how the CRM tool could connect people with the data they need. We realized we didn't really know what our users actually needed. Had we created a task force earlier, we could have saved ourselves valuable time and money wasted in implementing features we really didn't need."

Differentiation Barrier

A differentiation barrier in sustainable execution stems from the fact that getting the most benefit from 1 + 1 = 3 requires people to be both similar and different at the same time. Similarity holds a team together – common goals, values, and personalities make it easier to come to mutual agreement and understanding. On the other hand, differences between team members bring new perspectives and diverse opinions that discourage "group think" and inspire engagement and performance. Friction between people is typically associated with something negative – but in sustainable execution, differentiation adds vigor to the energy equation. The secret to why differentiation is helpful is that comparisons are needed to identify distractions that are preventing organizations from performing at their peak.

Sometime over the last decade or so, making comparisons between people or departments within organizations became socially unacceptable. Advice from highly successful people such as Bill Gates and Mary-Frances Winters to "not copy, compete with, or compare yourself to others" seems to have been marginalized as "good enough for me" or "I tried my hardest," as opposed to its original intent: bring your best self to the table. Without comparison, how do people or departments know their approach to execution is working or not working? Bluntly, there is such a thing as a bad customer in the context that some customers "cry wolf" to seek the discounts they want. This is not a judgment of the customer – it is a recognition that some customers may not be profitable. There are also underperforming products in the context of revenue generation. This is not to say the product is good or bad, it is just not selling in the context of other products and services the organization offers. Finally, there are underperformers in the context of employee productivity. Again, this is not to say they are lazy or incompetent, they are just not producing results at the same rate as others.

In sustainable execution, the trick to leveraging differentiation in a socially acceptable way is to make comparisons in context. Specifically, *avoid playing things safe*. Our research found 65 per cent of managers feel their organizations limit opportunities by playing things "safe," such as giving everyone a 5 per cent salary increase where there is clear evidence of variations in performance, or removing a reward because one or two people abused their privileges. A more specific example is a program that aimed to stimulate collaboration between health care and social service professionals to provide better care for patients with severe medical and social issues. The evaluation of program results offered some general insights, but the real opportunities for improvement came from comparing different approaches. When the evaluation was shared with key stakeholders, people got defensive and spent excessive time and energy justifying their approach. This brings us to the second source of a differentiation barrier: when organizations make comparisons *without explaining why differences are important (i.e., context)*. Perhaps if the program launched under the auspice that different approaches were encouraged and benefits would be compared without harm or penalty, stakeholders would have been less resistant. In the end, the evaluation was published without the comparisons, and the inability to differentiate prevented the most valuable lessons from being learned.

Isolation Barrier

Finally, nothing undermines collaboration more profoundly than isolation. Isolation occurs when departments or groups within an organization are unable or choose not to share information or knowledge with other individuals for a variety of reasons.

- Organizations operate across multiple time zones, languages, and cultures. The inability to communicate in a common language or differences in values and communication styles rooted in culture make it difficult to share information and knowledge. For example, a simple language barrier makes misunderstandings, irritations, feelings of exclusion, and a sense of inferiority a daily challenge.
- Departments and groups live in different silos on the organization chart. When silos are isolated, the term *collaboration* is often used loosely. Centralized steering committees, centers of excellence, and cross-functional teams are put in place to enable collaboration, but distractions arise as people are ultimately loyal to the demands of their department or line of business. Commonly referred to as "silo mentality," this is the most common source of isolation.
- Insider groups or "cliques" is another type of isolation that most commonly forms in corporate environments with weak management. Katherine Crowley and Kathi Elster, co-authors of *Working with You Is Killing Me*, equate these insider groups to "office

gangs that emerge to fill in the void of leadership."[7] Such cliques proactively conceal information and knowledge as a way to establish power. If not policed, they become problematic, as they create social pressure and develop their own set of rules for how people should behave.

- Finally, if you have ever lived through a merger or acquisition, you have likely experienced or witnessed isolation that forms when different cultures live in the same organization. Our research found this type of isolation barrier in 37 per cent of organizations. It causes execution to break down because independent cultures support and bolster their own initiatives and ideas, regardless of what is best for the organization as a whole. In fact, leaders involved in acquisitions describe the isolation between cultures as one of the biggest hurdles to overcome, as senior leaders who refuse to conform to the new approach to doing business often need to be either demoted or removed.

There are several ways to prevent isolation barriers from taking a stronghold. Making an extra effort to include newcomers, encouraging everyone's contribution, and changing longstanding reporting relationships is good leadership and essential for promoting synergy. However, once part of an organization is isolated, collaboration suffers, as vast amounts of skills, expertise, and knowledge remain hidden or lost.

Orchestrating the Collaboration Shift

Most organizations equate collaboration with the need to build high-performing, interdisciplinary teams. Certainly teams are very effective at orchestrating collaboration, but simply assigning teams to collaborative work is not sufficient. Organizations need to invest more time and energy in removing distractions that get in the way.

Recently scholars and practitioners have begun to explore ways organizations can collaborate beyond teams. In fact, researchers who study collaboration found surprising common ground with some of the most successful collaborators – they waste 50 per cent less time in meetings.[8] But how do they do it? We offer three modern orchestrations that may help.

Keep Collaboration Simple

Collaboration is a human tendency that will naturally evolve in most organizations when tools and techniques are kept simple.[9] Modernizing existing methods such as visual management,[10] standardized forms, policies, and procedures, and basic communication bring information sharing and cooperative action back to the basics. In fact one organization resisted the temptation to invest in a costly collaborative technology platform by recognizing five strategically placed whiteboards would have the same, or perhaps better, impact. Organizations need to recognize that any investment in technology will come at a cost of change. Either technology will need to be highly customized to emulate how people naturally collaborate and work together, or significant change management costs will be incurred to deal with resistance and frustration that comes from forcing people to collaborate in different ways.

If your organization has already invested in a shiny new collaborative platform and it is not being used to its fullest potential, seek to understand "why" the platform is not working. If senior leadership are not using it, that usually explains why the rest of the organization is not using it either. Also collaborative tools do not always make people's jobs easier. For example, requiring workers to enter information into a system (e.g., reporting, tracking) may seem necessary but also takes a lot of time and energy. As such, organizations need to explore simpler ways (e.g., "enter once, reuse often," voice-to-text) that make data entry less burdensome and time consuming.

Finally, global and highly dispersed companies can create a vibrant online social network to pull people together and encourage wonderful, insightful, and spontaneous connections. Online platforms are powerful collaboration tools, as technology can accommodate translation between multiple languages and is open and accessible 24/7. When organizations build a vibrant online community, McKinsey claims productivity between high-skilled knowledge workers will increase by 20 to 25 per cent[11] and the time employees spend searching for company information can be reduced by as much as 35 per cent. A well-known success story is Waste Management, the leading provider of comprehensive waste management and renewable energy generation services in North America. They use Twitter to communicate with employees during outages as well as other time-sensitive issues, and field agents use Yammer and SharePoint to access details and historical context about specific customers. Their social media platform operates in multiple languages, builds trust, and brings people together in ways not possible in the past.

Scrums and Workathons

Synergy can be orchestrated by redesigning organizational work – by setting aside traditional approaches that determine work units based on complexity and macro-level requirements, and replacing them with execution approaches that drive speed by leveraging people's ability to self-organize and solve complex problems. The most popular work design in today's organization is a framework for collaboration from the Agile project management domain that uses the "scrum" concept. Scrums are used to execute work in a productive and creative way with the intent to deliver the highest possible value. Although it found its roots in software development, a scrum is a framework that can be applied to any organizational activity (e.g., strategic planning, budgeting, etc.). The modern perspective promotes speed, transparency of key information, and flexibility in terms of enhancing opportunities for adaptation and change. Specifically, the artifacts of a scrum are as follows:

- A *single source of information* about the initiative is required to make sure people have access to the right information at the right time. This source needs to be living (i.e., never complete) and evolve through the lifetime of an activity. For example, in strategic planning this single source might be a backlog of ideas and notes describing why ideas were, or were not, included in the plan. As strategic planning cascades down the organization, multiple teams can use and add to this single source of information to enhance alignment, learn from others, and lower the risk of repeating past mistakes.
- Work is designed in *small increments* or batch sizes that produce something valuable or useable. In strategic planning, increments may be a series of two-day off-sites that start with a corporate strategic plan and follow up with a series of departmental off-site meetings. Reducing the size of work is a key way to deliver faster, cheaper, and better results for a variety of reasons, First, there are repetitive processes across work activities (e.g., ideation, planning), and smaller increments provide opportunities for people to gain experience. Next, people have an inherent tendency to work more efficiently and produce higher-quality work when approaching a deadline. Finally, when designing work in small increments, organizations create more opportunity for people to experience a sense of accomplishment and produce high quality, increasing both engagement and morale.
- If an organization is going to get something wrong, they need to do it early and *fail fast*. Recovery from a small mistake can be

managed with discretion, while delaying failure makes problems worse and can have catastrophic effects. Essential to failing fast is embedding regular review and relevant feedback that encourage people to show their work along the way. Feedback not only leads to course corrections, but there are many situations where something that worked yesterday will not necessarily work tomorrow. So the opportunity to look at work from multiple perspectives creates opportunities for improvement and helps to mitigate risk.

Designing work using a scrum framework is a particularly useful approach, as it transforms execution into a hum of activity that allows organizations to practice sharing information and making decisions to achieve a common purpose. In fact, many organizations are combining the scrum framework with other modern work designs to accelerate the benefits of collaboration. For example, a hackathon discussed earlier is a specific type of "workathon" that combines scrums with elements of game playing (e.g., point score, competition, play) in an effort to encourage creativity, productivity, and engagement. Hackathons are being held at businesses, schools, and community spaces all over the globe, with massive organizations like HP Inc., Google, and Facebook hosting their own internal ones. We encourage organizations to explore ways they can leverage the benefits of workathons as a pragmatic approach to orchestrating collaboration. Any type of work that can be accelerated to two or three days can reap similar benefits such as "paperathons" at academic conferences and "createathons" at marketing agencies. Our team worked with one organization that even transformed the budget process into a two-day event where everyone in the organization cleared their calendars and worked together to finalize the corporate budget. Leadership championed the initiative and branded it "Budget Days," complete with "budget day" T-shirts and cupcakes.

They were 100 per cent dedicated and involved and expected everyone to follow their example. Inspiration for the novel initiative came
from the insight that the iterative process of budgeting, although
important, often dragged on too long and consumed more time
and energy than necessary. Orchestrating collaboration in this way
did not come without its hiccups, but year-over-year budget day
improves, and the overall benefit to the organization far outweighs
the challenges experienced along the way.

Ventilating Silos

Shel Holtz, a principal of Holtz Communication + Technology,
challenges the feasibility of breaking down organizational silos.[12]
He recognizes the consequences of allowing silos to form, but also
highlights the need for silos to remain intact, as they are essential for
allocating resources efficiently and making sure the organization's
core competencies have a strategy and are structured into day-to-
day work. He claims that silos are not to blame, as the problem with
collaboration is not structure, it is that silos are not properly venti-
lated. Silo ventilation makes sure air moves in and out of the silo so
negative by-products (e.g., heat and humidity) can escape the silo,
and fresh resources (e.g., oxygen) are brought in. We've come across
a number of ways organizations can ventilate organizational silos
and share a few below:

• Have a common place where people gather to eat and socialize, but make sure no one is excluded from participating. An
  executive lunchroom is not a formal silo, but it certainly isolates
  executives from the rest of the organization. Similarly, a company golf tournament, baseball league, or weekly pub gatherings
  can be problematic if people are not comfortable playing sports
  or drinking alcohol.

- Cross-pollinate leadership and proactively move people from one department to another as much as pragmatically possible. There is a saying that all leaders or managers have a shelf life. This is not because they become less competent, it is because their approach becomes stale and outdated. By making transitions, organizations can also disrupt isolating behavior and create natural opportunities for synergy to emerge.
- Co-locating people to work on the same floor or building is very effective at ventilating silos. When people work in close proximity to one another, opportunities for communication and collaboration are enhanced and new opportunities and collaborative practices emerge.
- Finally, nothing ventilates a silo as effectively as encouraging difficult conversations. When distractions are at play, bringing the issues to everyone's attention, being open and honest about why they exist, and addressing them head-on will help them disappear. Silo mentality does not happen overnight; it escalates over time when small groups experience little to no consequence when they exclude others. Keeping an eye out for this behavior and addressing issues early is essential to ventilating silos. Unfortunately, our research shows that the need for difficult conversations significantly outweighs the number that are actually conducted.

Orchestrating collaboration to promote synergy requires organizations to coordinate with others, but in business it is not always possible to give everyone involved equal opportunity. In fact, in today's environment, companies need to engage in collaboration even when the direct value to them is not necessarily clear. We end this chapter with an example of collaboration that illustrates this point. For decades, standard business practices of the chocolate industry have had devastating effects, including reduction of rainforest cover of up to 80 per cent in areas of Africa. Unethical industry behavior opened up the industry to criticism as well as opportunities for new incumbents such as Tony's Chocolonely to enter the market by offering fair trade alternatives.[13] In 2013, Mars, the manufacturer of chocolate brands including M&M'S and Snickers, publicly voiced their intent to "right the wrongs." They initiated the CocoaAction strategy,[14] which formalized arrangements with NGOs, government, and direct competitors to mitigate harmful practices. With movements such as "conscious consumerism" and "corporate sustainability" continuing to grow, this is exactly the type of collaboration today's customers expect. So is this an example of promoting synergy? Absolutely yes. While mitigating the ethical concerns, Mars recognized that better farming practices could triple the yield of cocoa per hectare, making this a clear example of 1 + 1 = 3. Not only did they "do the right thing," their collaborative effort improved the sustainability of the industry's supply chain over the long term.[15]

6

SHIFT APTITUDE TO SUSTAIN FOCUS

The final shift deals with challenges of the day-to-day work that is at the heart of execution. Work demands create a whirlwind of activity that acts like a giant vacuum cleaner, effortlessly sucking up finite hours in a day. In sustainable execution, aptitude is the organization's ability to deliver consistent and predictable results by finding the optimal approach to work across different, and often competing business priorities. In 2011 McKinsey & Company conducted a survey of 1,374 global executives, and only 52 per cent said general managers and above spent time working on the most important strategic initiatives.[1] One year later, the Harris Poll found a similar result – only 49 per cent of people's time focused on achieving the company goals, while the rest was spent on urgent distractions.[2] Focusing day-to-day work is vital to delivering on the company's top goals and objectives, and on the basis of our research, we can confirm that few companies are doing anything about it. Precious work hours are mismanaged in 90 per cent of organizations; as such, the ability to sustain focus offers a substantial opportunity to improve execution.

Phone calls, emails, meetings, and teleconferences eat up hours in every manager's day, but companies do nothing to govern those interactions.[3] A shift in aptitude encourages organizations to invest in the reality that "time is money" and start finding ways to keep energy focused on work that drives results. A prerequisite for focus is clearly aligned goals, as they establish the backbone for what is deemed important when priorities become blurred by the tyranny of urgent work drivers in the "day job." Experts claim focusing time day in and day out accelerated the pace of innovation at companies such as Apple, helping them become one of the largest in the world by market capitalization. So how did they do it?

A pivotal engagement at a large branch of a Canadian bank uncovered the capabilities that make shifting aptitude distinct from other shifts in our model. The branch operated in a large Canadian city where keeping up to the speed of business was crucial for success. Our work with them started on the heels of the sub-prime real estate crisis,[4] as they had missed performance targets for mortgage products by 35 per cent year over year. Executives described it as a "systemic problem that we can't seem to fix no matter what we do." Our engagement eventually led us to interviews with customers where we repeatedly heard customers claim, "CanadaBank[5] just can't seem to do what needs to be done to make things happen." Most customers were aware of the bank's need to tighten up their controls after the sub-prime crisis, but low-risk customers did not expect their services to be affected. Also customers were not naive about the fact that processing a mortgage request was complicated, but to them – getting to a simple "Yes" or "No" and a set of terms were all they were looking for. One customer said, "When I called to inquire, the bank manager offered drivel about how complicated it was to process a mortgage application. The manager went on to provide additional meaningless information about how the credit department was missing some information on the application and that it was a very busy time for mortgages at the bank." In the end, while CanadaBank was busy explaining the distractions in their work, a smaller, local competitor found ways to comply with increased compliance regulations more efficiently so they could continue to satisfy the needs of the customer. In both banks, risk mitigation and enhancing the customer experience were clear priorities; however, the day-to-day realization of those priorities played out in very different ways.

What Is Focus?

We add focus to our energy analogy by demonstrating that a shift in aptitude enables the organization to recognize and reduce distractions to redirect time and energy to the most productive uses. A lack in focus is dangerous, as energy is permitted to travel along unintended paths, causing waste or "leakage." Many managers feel a decrease in focus is caused by people being assigned too much responsibility or "spread too thin." We do not disagree; however, in our Shift-to-Execute framework, setting realistic goals and objectives is more about filling gaps in resource allocation and alignment than it is about focus. In this chapter, the energy leak we are addressing is the inability to ground every task and focus every hour of work on what is most important. When focus is lacking, employees lose the autonomy they need to do their job and struggle to find the optimal path to results. This struggle results in working harder, as the giant vacuum cleaner of activity exhausts time and energy without people being clear about how their endless effort is making a difference.

Shifting "aptitude" involves establishing appropriate controls that guide behavior and eliminate distractions, enabling people to find the optimal path to do their best work, and getting beyond experience, assumptions, and rituals that may hold a company back. Organizations can learn to use this shift by considering four capabilities that help organizations stay focused on value-added work. First, the organization needs to become comfortable with the fact

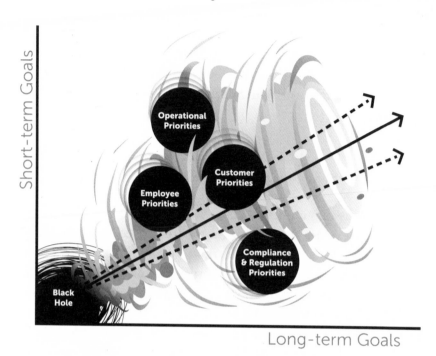

Figure 6.1 Sustainable Execution Approach to Shift Aptitude

that their *focus often needs to adjust, as priorities (circles) of stakeholders (i.e., customer, employee) and business units (i.e., operational, compliance) differ, depending on specific situations.* Figure 6.1 shows that priorities vary according to the short-term (i.e., quarterly revenue targets, resolution of quality, customer service issues) and long-term (profitability, growth, infrastructure, employee retention, productivity) demands of the business. To illustrate using an example, consider an employee at CanadaBank processing a mortgage for a customer who is purchasing a home with multiple competitive offers. In this situation, the priority for both the customer and employee is urgency to close the deal; however, the employee also needs to follow internal risk-assessment procedures. The operational priority is to drive revenue and provide efficient customer service, and the compliance priority is to mitigate longer-term risk. The whirlwind in figure 6.1 represents the day-to-day work that attempts to deliver on all competing priorities of the business.

Second, shifting aptitude recognizes that *priorities (circles) may move to drive work differently across situations.* What worked for one customer last week may not work for a different customer this week. Returning to the CanadaBank example, if the risk assessment identifies the customer as low risk, the priority for compliance should become less important to the specific situation. The challenge is the plethora of different workflows, policies, and procedures that dictate how urgent requirements and different priorities are translated across various stakeholders and departments. When the controls in these procedures are too tight, priorities (circles) are more difficult to move, creating a distraction and slowing down work. As the employee at CanadaBank explained, "In my old bank, if my branch manager told me to expedite a mortgage application because the customer was low risk and purchasing a home with multiple competitive offers, getting credit manager approval was easy. However, here I lose valuable customers all the time as the approval process slows things right down. In CanadaBank, the risk profile of a customer doesn't seem to carry the same weight, making it difficult to close deals in fast-moving real estate markets." Failing to manage customer priorities was a primary reason that mortgage products missed targets by 35 per cent year over year.

Third, an organization's attempts to focus work may often face competing priorities. When one size does not fit all, people need *training, authority, and latitude to determine how to best fit[6] their work according to the needs of specific situations.* Illustrated by the arrow in figure 6.1, the best fit for a specific situation is a trade-off across multiple stakeholder priorities (circles). Experience in managing this trajectory of best fit strengthens a manager's ability to execute.

Often those best at execution are said to be "creative problem-solvers" who have a "sixth sense" of what problems need to be nipped in the bud before they happen. Finding the best fit in each situation also requires the latitude to make exceptions to policy or procedure if necessary. Managers also need training, authority, and latitude to systematically view each situation as a unique set of conditions that must be navigated and satisfied, as well as recognize and avoid pitfalls along the way. Take for example, another employee at CanadaBank who explained, "I've learned the best approach to getting approvals expedited here is to get both managers on the phone. I expect doing this too much could cause problems so I take this approach only when absolutely necessary." It takes skilled and competent employees to know when it is appropriate to set up a call and when it is not; specifically, essential to aptitude is an employee's ability to use corporate procedures and policies in the way they are intended.

Finally, the ability to maintain focus also comes from making sure the short- and long-term value of all initiatives is clearly defined so potential *"black hole" initiatives or executive-level pet projects* do not create distraction. Such distractions occur in 53 per cent of organizations, according to our research. We uncovered a "black hole" initiative at a well-known insurance company that resonates well with organizations that struggle in this regard. The CEO had worked in conjunction with a major IT vendor to implement a new customer-centric processing (rate, quote, issue resolution) platform. The idea was completely supported by the CIO but no one else in the C-suite. Four years were spent finding ways to work the new system into the day-to-day routine. Time and energy were wasted on workarounds and efforts to get people to change and buy in to the new system. After millions of dollars were invested and the CEO retired, the organization removed the system and returned to their old way of doing things. When speaking with the CFO who joined the organization two years prior to the CEO's retirement, he stated, "We would have obtained far more value by reconfiguring our legacy systems and using all that money to increase our staff." As in this example, organizations need to acknowledge and shift focus away from black hole initiatives as soon as they are recognized. This example also highlights that the drive for sustained focus must be supported from the highest levels in the organization.

Through our research we learned that shifting aptitude to sustain focus in the daily whirlwind of activity is the most dynamic and challenging shift in sustainable execution, and it works most effectively when the barriers in the previous shifts have been addressed. By developing these four capabilities, organizations will significantly improve their ability to deliver short-term results while keeping long-term needs top of mind.

Barriers to Sustaining Focus

Infusing priorities into the daily whirlwind of activity gives employees the ability to make sound trade-offs and deliver better results. They will become more readily able to identify high-priority work and avoid distractions when they arise. We define three common barriers to focus in our sustainable execution model.

Control Barrier

Control barriers stem from organizational policies, procedures, and controls that lose sight of why they were established in the first place. Recall the new order system at Games and Entertainment Galore (GEG) discussed in chapter 2. To control the use of packaging material, the system predetermined the size of box for each order, and management tracked compliance between packaging material and order size as a way to monitor warehouse productivity. Although the intention behind this control was to reduce packaging waste, there were times it was counterproductive when put into operation. Five large boxes packed to the brim with polystyrene packing peanuts satisfied the metric in the control system; however, the customer was left perplexed and concerned about the environmental impact of GEG's practices. This was one of the fourteen controls GEG removed to improve their execution systems. In sustainable execution, 49 per cent of managers agree their organizations have mandatory policies and procedures in place that result in counterproductive work. Avoiding this type of control barrier requires the organization to "right-size" controls for effectiveness and train people how to implement the control that is impeding business value.

Another source of a control barrier are "nice-to-have" policies and procedures that leadership put in place on the basis of their own needs, or preferences for how work "should" be done. For example, one organization required human resources to print off detailed reports of all top talent in the company. Creating these reports was exhaustive, as leadership said they wanted to know everything or anything they might deem important in their upcoming talent meetings. Reports for all employees were printed, divided into sections, and put in three-inch binders. In the talent meetings, reports for the first fifteen to twenty names that required immediate attention were reviewed and discussed; however, many binders were not even opened. Some binders were even left on the table at the end of the meeting. Eventually, a newly appointed vice president of HR brought this to the attention of the leadership. As soon as they were made aware, the rationale for putting a stop this approach made complete sense. In sustainable execution, such a distraction highlights the harm of "busy work" on productivity – the "nice-to-have" duties that distract valuable time and energy away from the organization's most important goals and objectives.

Finally, organizations are encouraged to recognize that effective use of control is a paradox – *the more control you have, the less control they need*. Forcing people to jump through hoops or get approval when they are accountable for results is a significant waste of energy. Allowing controls to be used inappropriately not only slows productivity down, it strips people of the authority they need to do their job. Generating a status report that no one reads and tracking metrics that are not acted upon are a waste of valuable energy.

Prioritization Barrier

In the day-to-day whirlwind of activity, urgent work will always take precedence over important work, causing prioritization barriers to arise. Professionals such as lawyers and accountants who treat "time as money" and bill their fees accordingly create focus by putting hard numbers on time. Assuming the average professional in an organization drives an annual expense of $100,000 a year, a one-hour meeting involving six people should generate at least $300 in value.[7] If only ten minutes of meeting are productive, the meeting created $50 of value and $250 of waste. Organizations that do not talk about time in terms of money, waste time on urgent but not meaningful distractions and are more susceptible to exhausting and overwhelming their workforce with non-value added work.

It is also imperative that changing priorities across stakeholders and business units are effectively communicated so departments and individuals know how adjusted priorities affect their day-to-day work. Our research found 72 per cent of organizations fail to do this, causing a prioritization barrier to arise. In most cases, such a prioritization barrier stems from ineffective communication and/ or unclear accountability. Take an operational expense reduction as an example. A carefully crafted company-wide email needs to let the organization know there is an issue and set the expectation that all need to do their part. The email creates awareness, but follow-up is needed to establish the urgency and accountability to connect the priority to people's day-to-day practice. Managers who check in with their employees one-on-one to discuss ways they can reduce expenses will establish a heightened commitment to doing so. In addition, when leadership state a change in priority, they must adjust their own behavior to set a good example.

Next, priorities need to be validated in a way that individuals deem the priority important in their day-to-day work. For example, most organizations have a high-level priority that relates to employee motivation and validate that priority once a year through an employee engagement survey. The effectiveness of the validation approach is important to prioritization; is this a good approach to measuring employee engagement? Is once a year sufficient? Also many organizations further validate the priority by assigning a percentage of leadership's compensation plan to the results of the employee engagement survey. Forty per cent of managers in our research say they get frustrated in their job because they are held accountable for high-level results where they control and influence only a small part of the process. As such, it is important for organizations to recognize that linking an outcome like employee engagement to compensation plans for the senior management team may be effective to establish the right culture across the organization.

Finally, to prioritize effectively, people need to stop equating "focus" to being more organized and merely starting each day with a clear "to do" list. Finding the optimal path to deliver results entails analyzing trade-offs across competing priorities to determine "how" work will be done to complement their list of "to dos." Also, people too often turn to their boss to resolve competing priorities.

While the boss is there to assist on occasion, all employees need to be able to think critically and have the freedom to find the optimal path to driving their own work results, as they are the one closest to the work.

Insularity Barrier

The final barrier is another hidden element of execution caused by deep-rooted cultural issues and assumptions that underlie industry norms, core competencies, and values that drive everyday behavior. In sustainable execution, insularity is the ignorance or lack of interest in trends, ideas, or people outside one's own experience. This barrier was uncovered by one result in our research that many organizational leaders find difficult to digest – only 27 per cent of people feel leadership dedicates sufficient time and energy to understand what is truly going on. At the heart of the insularity barrier is the fact that people are inherently trapped in their own assumptions, don't communicate effectively, and sometimes fail to speak the whole truth. When multiple people are assigned the same task or responsibility, distractions from assumptions are inevitable. Let's go back to the status report that no one reads. Although a status report is generated, a leader may assume the project manager will alert her on a timely basis via email or a phone call when there is a problem. However, a project manager likely assumes the leader has read the report and only needs to alert her about additional issues that arise. In this simple example, both parties are trapped by their own assumptions, causing a "disconnect" and issues left unaddressed until they become a bigger problem. Both parties' assumptions contributed to the problem; such a distraction saturates the whirlwind of daily activity in many organizations.

Another source of an insularity barrier are the assumptions inherent in the organization's past experience that define their position in the industry and those companies with whom they compete. Many experts claim the corporate world is in the midst of a revolution – quantum leaps in technology are making organizations vulnerable as a result of the exponential growth in the speed of business. Claims such as "no company owns their market share, they are simply renting it" speak to the need for organizations to be more aware of their surroundings and willing to adjust their assumptions about who they are and how they compete. In *Sense and Respond*, Jeff Gothelf and Josh Seiden highlight a new universal skill they define as *"listening, assessment, and response."*[8] Our research confirms this skill is extremely rare – only 17 per cent of managers strongly agree that people in their organization listen well, and critically assess risks and new information to challenge assumptions, perspectives, or previous approaches to focusing work. It calls attention to the importance of the role that industry awareness, good judgment, and open-mindedness play in driving the need to continuously adapt and change.

Next, no one can expect others to be mind-readers. We worked with one CEO who had observed employees investing endless time and energy searching online for optimum flight schedules for their own business travel, but when they were asked to find a document or piece of information, their attention span reduced to minutes. At the core of his frustration was the observation that employees are wrapped up in their own priorities. He used words like *entitlement, self-centeredness*, and *narcissism* to describe today's workforce. We asked him to tell us some stories about real situations when this occurred. As we listened, we realized that in the situations he described, the information he requested was relevant to something extremely important to him. We explained that employees may spend more time and energy if he clearly articulates the importance of the information and what purpose it would serve. To paraphrase his response, he felt the fact that he was CEO should mean every information request was important, which pointed to yet another insularity barrier sometimes inherent in those with authority.

When leadership burdens employees with "nice-to-have," and "need-to-know" demands, they need to be honest about the fact that these requests create distractions for people in their organization. We recognize that authoritative or "nice-to-have" requests may occasionally be necessary, but to achieve sustainable execution, leaders must be forthright about the nature of these requests, otherwise trust will be lost. The 2017 Edelman Trust Barometer found that only 37 per cent describe CEOs as credible spokespeople, down from 49 per cent in 2016. Forty-eight per cent found fellow employees trustworthy, down from 52 per cent in 2016. Finally, the majority of global respondents say they no longer trust "the system" (i.e., government, media, business, and institutions) to work for them.[9] Removing the insularity barrier has the greatest positive impact on trust. When those with the most power and influence become aware of how their assumptions and behavior set the example and tolerance level for creating distractions, execution significantly improves. Trust in the organization reduces the time that people spend looking over their shoulder or taking action to protect themselves and justify their actions.

Orchestrating the Focus Shift

Sixty-eight per cent of managers in our research disagreed that their organization helped eliminate distractions that suck time, attention, and energy away from delivering results. So what can organizations do? The first thing organizations need to realize is that no one is intentionally doing work that drives limited value; it is just the way things tend to play out in the whirlwind of daily activity. Figure 6.2 illustrates how some distractions are inherent in common business practice, such as segregation of duties and integrating work across departments and organizations (i.e., service integration). Third-party oversight and compliance with regulatory requirements are other seemingly justified distractions. Our research found 66 per cent of

Figure 6.2 The Unfortunate Reality of Today's Work

managers feel government regulation, third-party influence, and soci-
etal demands have increased approvals and procedure to the point
that they no longer feel they have the control they need to do their
job. According to Protiviti's 2016 Sabanes Oxley Compliance Survey,
the average company's internal costs of compliance are well over
$1 million per year – and over $2 million for companies with more than
$20 billion of revenue.[10] Finally, distraction overload from cell phones
and social media is an unfortunate reality that's here to stay.

As such, orchestrating focus in the day-to-day work environment
can be exceptionally challenging, but we offer a few practices that
may help.

Delegate Accountability

Essential to maintaining focus is a recognition that when operational planning and budgets cascade down the organization, clear priority and accountability need to follow. Organizations need to delegate accountability for work to the right levels of the organization. For example, once the CFO has approved the annual capital plan and revalidated the cash expenditure in advance of each quarter, approving each purchase order should be delegated to someone further down in the financial organization. The need to approve each purchase order not only creates a distraction in excess work, it can be perceived as lack of trust or excessive control amongst the leadership team.

Delegating accountability is one of the most important managerial tasks. It is imperative that the person or team assigned to do the task has:

- A clear understanding of what success looks for all stakeholders;
- Appropriate transparency of financial information to manage priorities based on how the organization makes money and/or defines value;
- Decision authority to take appropriate action, and knowledge about when approval is needed; and
- The training and latitude to understand the situational aspects of the work and determine the best fit across all priorities.

Even when accountability to do the work is delegated, the ultimate accountability for results stays with the manager. So we suggest the following managerial oversight:

- Include all stakeholders in regular checkpoints to gain a 360-degree view of progress and to keep priorities in check so work can focus on the best fit.

- When appropriate, let your team experience failure and provide them with guidance and feedback so they can learn from their mistakes.
- Keep your perceptions in check; those who demand the most and yell the loudest are not necessarily the ones who will generate the most benefit from your attention.

Finally, when accountability is delegated, there needs to be an inherent agreement that resources will continue to flow as if the person doing the work personally. For example, if the manager has a well-established internal and external network, the delegate should be able to leverage that network when appropriate to move work along and navigate checkpoints to drive people to action. If managers have expertise, they need to take the time to share their knowledge and transfer their skills. If managers have access to resources (people, money) they would use if they were doing the work, they need to make them available. The main point here is that delegating accountability is about mentoring and coaching, not abdication. Coaching is the structured and formal approach to guiding work over a shorter period of time, and mentoring is a long-term process that builds mutual trust and respect.

Remove Talent Bottlenecks

To deliver on the competing priorities of the business, competent and well-trained people are essential. Talent bottlenecks are caused by a number of issues, and organizations that proactively remove them are more effective at sustaining focus. The first issue is that hiring processes are strained and often too slow to keep pace with the speed of business. Although finding the right talent requires rigor, organizations need to make sure their hiring approach is not holding the organization back. Lengthy, burdensome recruitment

processes often lose excellent candidates to organizations who realize the need to expedite a rigorous search more quickly. Vetting candidates needs to be balanced with swift action to secure the best
talent before a competitor does so. Hiring based on quotas to satisfy
targets for diversity and other workforce expectations is also problematic, as many leaders equate diversity with hiring ethnic minori-
ties, women, and those from lower-income backgrounds. Getting
true diversity in the workplace takes years, as it requires access to
tools and resources that not only hire a diverse workforce but also
eliminate discriminatory employment barriers. Sufficient investment of time, energy, and resources is needed to remove this type of
talent bottleneck.

In addition to hiring, promotion and termination procedures
that are decentralized, under-scrutinized, and non-collaborative
can inadvertently create costly talent bottlenecks. Tenure-based
advancement to management is the norm in many organizations
and, according to Gallup, organizations get it wrong 82 per cent of
the time.[11] Only one in ten people possess the necessary talent to
manage well, and tenure does not equate to having the ability to lead
others and sustain a culture of high productivity. Using promotion
to increase retention rates is also bad practice; denying a promotion
may inspire a change that is best for both the person and the organization. Moving fast to correct a bad hire or replace a bad leader is
also important, especially in those positions higher up in the organization. This is not always a criticism of one's ability, and more often
it is about the right fit. If an organization is pursuing new strategic
territory, a visionary leader may be more effective. However, if an
organization is heading into a period of financial constraints, the talent of a visionary leader may be better served elsewhere.

The next bottleneck that needs to be addressed is finding talent that
have the skills needed to make appropriate trade-offs and optimize
work. Research shows 92 per cent of American executives believe

workers are under-skilled.[12] The deficiency is not limited to technical skills. Today's employees lack universal hard and soft skills such as writing, public speaking, and data analysis needed to effectively do their job. PayScale[13] confirms five critical skills that are lacking in today's graduates.[14] *Critical thinking* and *problem-solving* skills are important to find optimal approaches to work and remove everyday obstacles. *Attention to detail* makes sure multiple perspectives have been considered and work is thorough and accurate. Good *communication* is vital for understanding the inherent opportunities and risks across competing priorities. Recall the opportunity for the employee at CanadaBank to pick up the phone to process the mortgage application; if that employee lacked communication skills, even with latitude he may not have been inclined to make the call. Finally, *teamwork* is essential for navigating multiple agendas, as team skills help leverage the strengths offered by each team member, resolve conflicts, and see things through to completion.

The final way to remove a talent bottleneck is to improve people's insight into the fact that no matter what department or business unit they serve, their work affects the overall impression and opinion that stakeholders have of your company. Their actions create what the customer sees. Recall the discussion of Games Unlimited in chapter 2 where two divisions (online and in-store) end up in unhealthy competition for power, influence, and resources. Managers explained that ultimately the customers paid the price, as there were many complaints about the disconnect between shopping through the online channel and in-store services. As such, employees need to remain acutely aware of how their actions and decisions affect others in the value chain. If you are a Seinfeld fan, you may recall the episode where Jerry differentiates between "making" and "holding" a car rental reservation. His attempt to pick up a rental car fails because the company took his reservation, but as the agent explains, "Unfortunately, we ran out of cars." Jerry's comic diatribe articulately explains how customer value lies in holding the reserving – not taking it: "You know how to *take* the reservation, you just don't know how to *hold* the reservation – and that really is the most important part of the reservation, the holding."[15] In this example, overbooking reservations is a financial strategy to mitigate risk of cancellation and maximize profit. However, when all customers show up, the company resorts to policies and procedures to explain and justify their actions. Therefore, even though Finance do not have to deal with the customer directly, they still need to pay attention to the broader impact of their work. Overbooking is definitely a profitable goal for business, but as evident in Seinfeld's experience, lack of talent can be detrimental to business.

Proactively Manage Distractions

In a world full of distractions, it is easy to lose sight of the small things organizations can do to make a big difference. In 2016 the average executive sent and received an average of 121 emails each day – a number expected to increase by 16 per cent each year.[16] The effect of the "always on, always connected" world in which we live is a constant distraction. As such, organizations are encouraged to explore ways they embrace distractions by proactively managing them in ways to enhance focus. Communication channels in general (emails, texts, memos, hallway discussions, telephone calls, meetings, etc.) are prone to creating distractions, and organizations that are proactive at encouraging and adhering to communication plans for workflows, projects, and initiatives enforce the most productive channel for each purpose. Proactive redirection is required to ensure all parties get what they need – a hallway ambush may work for the person trying to get a quick signature, but signees may wish to redirect the request to a meeting to give more mindshare to what they are approving. Though there may be urgent exceptions, communications should not routinely create distractions to getting work done. A tolerance for distractions breeds more distractions.

Social media and YouTube are often deemed the biggest distraction; however, some companies are finding novel ways to use this technology to sustain focus. FlipGrid is a good example. "Grids" are ninety-second videos that spark discussion, share perspectives, and reflect on learning together. Replacing the traditional slide deck with a ninety-second video transforms burdensome presentations into short briefings that are efficient and easy to consume. When people are distracted by interesting work-related content, revolutionary approaches to corporate training and customer support will emerge.

Another approach to proactively managing distractions was inspired by our finding that many organizations experimenting with different time-management practices still suffered from *procrastination* – attention to a task being delayed or postponed – and *perfectionism* – attention to a task being overextended and wasteful. When it comes to execution, effective management of day-to-day routine keeps progress moving and work focused on the most important priorities. Some examples of proactively managing distractions include:

- Create, manage, and monitor shorter-term milestones to make sure people focus limited hours on achieving the most important goals and objectives;
- Say no to work initiatives that are unaligned with the agreed priorities;
- Do daily check-ins or establish a daily management[17] routine to make sure day-to-day work stays focused on current priorities;
- Escalate delays in open, transparent, and urgent ways so boards and senior leadership teams can offer help in removing obstacles;

- Give regular "pats on the back" so employees understand what the boss deems valuable; and
- Finally, create a standing agenda item to allow the leaders at all levels to reinforce and provide a regular update on those things that are really important for that business or division at that specific time. This does not require PowerPoint materials or documents; it is just an honest expression of what people can do to make the biggest difference.

In conclusion, distractions are inevitable in the accelerating whirlwind of day-to-day responsibilities. Every organization is susceptible to becoming a giant vacuum cleaner, effortlessly sucking up finite hours in a day. Minimizing the effects of overwork and stress is essential to sustainable execution, and building an aptitude for execution helps organizations clearly communicate their priorities, direct efforts to meaningful work, and manage realistic expectations. When organizations shift focus to increase aptitude, they reduce unproductive work, build trust, and ensure everyone's efforts contribute toward the achievement of goals.

PART FOUR

The Sustainable Execution Leader

The final section of the book, part four, wraps up our sustainable execution story by examining the leadership traits that are unique to those who are most successful at driving results in the short term without compromising the long-term sustainability of the company. By shifting our attention from the organization to the execution leader, we explore the impact of personal leadership as a source of energy that builds and energizes the organization as well as a source of friction or drag that holds back progress and wears down resources. This part of the book was inspired by two primary observations. First, leaders drive results in different ways. Some are great at setting a strategy and inspiring performance, but lose sight of the tactics that drive results. Some are very effective at creating urgency and high pressure to perform but not the best at building a culture for retaining employees in the longer term. The second observation is that organizations can invest significant time and resources in improving their execution system but continue to struggle when poor leadership is in place. In fact, a bad leader with sufficient power and influence can cripple an organization's execution system. By identifying and describing traits unique to effective execution leadership, our intent is to help organizations assess the ability of their current leadership team to drive results and make changes in leadership if necessary. Readers may also use this final section as a way to reflect on some of their own behaviors to assess their execution leadership strengths and where they may be driving a higher cost of execution than necessary.

7

THE ROLE OF LEADERSHIP IN SUSTAINABLE EXECUTION

One of the first questions we ask organizations that have experienced execution failure is "Who is accountable for execution?" We find that after some reflection and finger pointing the discussion often settles on "It depends who you ask." For example, if disjointed operations are the source of customer irritation, the spotlight falls on operations. Failures in automation are blamed on technology. Internal execution challenges in employee retention shine the spotlight on human resources. If we allow the conversation to go long enough, responsibility ultimately extends to the CEO. Assigning accountability for execution is difficult for two primary reasons.

- First, the only way one person can be held accountable is if the execution is in a vacuum: just the individual and the task with no other influences. Those able to get results by doing everything themselves are not execution leaders.
- Second, execution leadership exists across all levels of the organization, and ineffective leadership at one level impedes other leaders in their drive for results.

As such, we define an execution leader as anyone in the organization responsible for leading others to deliver on a business outcome.

Whether through a direct reporting relationship or less formal sphere of influence, execution leaders execute new strategies, transformative initiatives, acquisitions, new product or service launches, IT projects, cost-reduction initiatives, or a line of business responsible for running the day-to-day operations. So how do you recognize the actions of an execution leader? Successful execution leaders will uphold what is right and just, even if it is inconvenient or difficult. They will simplify the many moving parts of the business to make things clear and easy to understand. They will direct all energy to support a single corporate agenda, maintaining a zero tolerance level for tangential or personal agendas. They will build and nurture a network, both within and outside their line of business, to ensure they can seek support when needed, connect the dots, engage all minds, and understand the "bigger" picture. Finally, they will engage and fully utilize every resource at their disposal by creating an environment of trust and objectivity and in the end accomplish what they set out to do.

We defined the unique traits that differentiate execution leaders from other leaders in the organizations by analyzing behaviors using the same structure, rhythm, and awareness levers used to resolve execution barriers. By extending the balancing act concept to leadership, we uncovered unique traits that define leaders most capable of driving results in the short term without compromising the long-term success of the company – in other words, leaders most capable of sustainable execution.

Recall that in chapter 1 we made the claim that the balancing act of these three levers transforms leadership behaviors into the likes of a conductor of an orchestra who performs a balancing act to unify performers. The conductor gives real-time instructions when it is time to tone down the trumpets so the flutes can make their impact. The most influential leaders in our research were those who were brought in time and time again to clean up an organizational "mess" left by a predecessor or launch an important transformation initiative. They had a proven ability to get things done in challenging situations and an innate ability to execute under conditions such as limited talent, tight time lines, or high risk of failure. Consistent with the thousands of books written about the traits that define a strong leader, these people were effective communicators, skilled at listening, delegated responsibly, made sound decisions, inspired others, etc. However, they also demonstrated three unique traits that ensured they delivered on their commitments all the time, every time. No excuses. Organizations that put leaders with these traits into key execution roles were most capable of lowering their cost of execution and sustaining performance. The following sections describe the three most important traits of the sustainable execution leader.

Fortitude

It is often said that "execution is not for the faint of heart." The term *fortitude* is sometimes used synonymously with *perseverance, courage,* or *endurance*; however, all of these elements and more are inherent in fortitude. Leaders with fortitude have the *mental and emotional strength to live outside your comfort zone and do what is essential every time, even if it is inconvenient or difficult to do so.* Leaders with fortitude are most effective at avoiding or breaking down structural execution barriers such as resource allocation issues, organizational alignment, integration gaps, and inappropriate controls. Let's take a look at a scenario involving an executive (Joe) and two directors (Pat and Sam). Pat had been at the organization for several years and Sam was recently hired to explore unexamined territory or "white space" in order to identify new customers and drive sales growth. Joe was involved in several engagements where Sam introduced a growth opportunity (i.e., a new idea, client), and Pat would quickly claim ownership of the space or cite previous work on the subject. Being new to the team, Sam acquiesced to Pat's claim of ownership and moved on to the next potential idea. The problem was that Pat failed to follow up with action or yield results, causing growth opportunities to be abandoned. Joe allowed several cycles of the situation to repeat, leaving potential growth opportunities unexplored and no progress on the growth agenda. Let's examine specific traits of fortitude to further explore this scenario.

- **Take Appropriate Risk.** Although Sam was new, she persevered and continued to bring growth opportunities to the table, despite Pat's behavior. She was hired to change business models and kept her head up to challenge the status quo, as new opportunities were necessary for achieving success. People with fortitude take risks from a position of stability. This means they carefully think through related opportunities and threats and only pursue risk that has clear benefit and payback for the company. Sam was realistic in evaluating the feasibility of her ideas and had the strength to walk away when appropriate.
- **Utilize Candor.** Although Joe had witnessed several cycles, he never created the opportunity for a frank and honest conversation. The behavior was in plain sight and he chose not to address it. Sugarcoating messages at any level of the organization creates distractions that are counterproductive to execution. When there is candor, leaders' actions are aligned with their messages, making it easier for people to make sense of what they see going on in their environment. When teams have a leader who infuses candor at regular touchpoints by offering truthful and direct feedback, people are less surprised by decisions and more prepared to handle adversity.
- **Set Clear Boundaries.** The first time Pat claimed ownership of the space or cited previous work on the subject, Joe may not have

felt the need to ask for clarification about how the opportunity would be realized. However, the second time it happened, had Joe inquired about the status of the first opportunity he would have established clear boundaries between the directors. Saying no, or being explicit in who will take responsibility for what, is inherent in fortitude. Strong execution leaders reinforce their decisiveness by reassuring that there is enough work and opportunity for everyone to create value and move the company forward.

- **Relinquish Control.** Finally, leaders with fortitude are not hesitant to relinquish their control when it facilitates greater focus and achieves a better outcome. Sam acquiesced her control numerous times and moved on to the next idea. However, Pat was unable to relinquish control, even when resources to deliver were lacking; this was not right or just in terms of supporting the growth agenda.

So what leader displays the most fortitude? Pat was not willing to let go of any piece of the pie, and Joe turned a blind eye to the repeating dilemma. Both allowed opportunities to be neutralized at the expense of the organization's growth. Neither was willing to live outside the comfort zone but it was Joe who failed to do what was essential. Once Sam picked up on Joe's lack of fortitude to manage the growth objectives explicit in the company's strategy, it made sense to her why several capable predecessors had short tenures in the same role and had moved on to senior roles in other companies. She decided to do likewise.

Resolute

Successful execution leaders are committed to using all energy purposefully and are resolute in *maintaining zero tolerance for any activity that strays from the corporate agenda.* They are admirably purposeful, determined, unwavering, and capable of addressing rhythm-related barriers in sustainable execution. Specifically, they make sure the organization is constantly challenged by creating healthy pressure to perform, are consistent in their approach, are willing to differentiate how people and products are delivering on the corporate agenda, and are explicitly clear in stating the most important priorities for the business. When leaders are not resolute, they permit energy to divert away from the most important goals and objectives articulated in the company's strategy. To examine the traits associated with resolute leaders, we share a story about a company amidst the launch of a new financial system that included mandatory deliverables for both IT and Finance. The vice presidents from each department worked closely with Dhillon, the program lead for the financial system transformation, to deliver results.

- **Know Your Plan.** Dhillon was very clear about his plan and budget and consistent in sharing and communicating key metrics to project stakeholders and involving them in the pursuit. His monthly meetings were purposeful in that he quickly analyzed the past month's performance and forecasted ahead to identify opportunities to eliminate waste and ensure preparedness to absorb change. He knew precisely what was accounted for in the plan and budget and what was *not* included so that potential exposures were identified early. By sensitizing others to the plan and keeping it in the forefront, he allowed both departments to be watchful for unplanned impacts and risks and work together to generate alternatives.
- **Exploit What You've Got.** Dhillon was extremely resourceful in working within the project budget. He differentiated between what he wanted and what was actually needed every step of the way. If he wanted his team to prepare ten slides for a presentation, he'd reflect on what was actually needed and cut that down

to three or four when appropriate. He was able to absorb and understand the information provided and very accomplished in presenting and effectively delivering a message, using what his team prepared for him. Dhillon also rarely asked his team for changes unless there was clear payback and never blamed lack of resources or constraints as inhibitors to execution. He had worked with other leaders who wasted resources by saying things like, "I can't start that project without the custom software to track expenditures." "I can't utilize that warehouse space until the dock cameras are installed." "I can't meet with that client until the prototype is available." He preferred to make progress through incremental wins, make do with what he had, and ask for more only when absolutely necessary.

- **Simplify.** When we asked Dhillon's boss about his most admirable quality, she said it was his ability to bring diverse agendas of multiple parties together and simplify the "big picture" to solve problems and deliver on the most important priorities. He was vigilant in moving things forward and could identify when a personal or political agenda was at play. Dhillon could even dissipate unproductive issues involving his superiors, as he had an inherent ability to bringing the discussion back to the priorities and moving the project forward. His intolerance for "nice-to-haves" and personal preferences that redirected energy away from work priorities was evident in his day-to-day behavior.

- **Differentiate.** Dhillon was very aware of the competing priorities between IT and Finance and leveraged healthy contention to drive optimum trade-offs. He had regular one-on-ones with the vice presidents from each group so he could understand their boundaries, make efficient handoffs, and eliminate overlaps in managing the project tasks. By recognizing that each unit needed to remain in control of their boundaries, being clear about how their needs were similar and different allowed him to manage the project in a way that contributed the most benefit to the overall corporate agenda.

- **Prioritize.** Finally, Dhillon was steadfast in making sure resources were focused on the right things every day and his own actions reinforced the need to find the optimal fit across competing priorities. His team understood they could not be involved in setting all the goals, but Dhillon was very good at explaining the game plan and how stakeholder priorities differed. Being explicit in this way prevented distractions from mixed messages and reduced the likelihood of people wasting time on lower-value work.

As the result of Dhillon's resolute leadership, his team was protected from undue stress and overlapping boundaries and deliverables. Throughout the project, both IT and Finance were satisfied and confident that progress was being made. Even though people were juggling many day-to-day responsibilities, they rarely found themselves at a crossroad, but if they did, they knew what to do. Throughout our research, it was common to hear people ask: "Why do some of my peers have different or more information than I do?" "Why am I hearing one message from our CEO, but the actions I am witnessing do not reflect that agenda?" These questions arise when leaders fail to formalize and set a consistent tempo for communicating priorities and why they change. Dhillon was very cognizant of the fact that his actions spoke louder than his words when it came to leadership and his zero tolerance approach minimized energy lost.

Accessible

Being accessible is a conscious choice that each one of us makes. We all receive phone calls that we'd rather not answer when we see who is calling. In sustainable execution, accessible leaders have an inherent ability to *"pay attention" to what is really going on, mitigate risks, and sense and exploit new opportunities.* They are very effective at breaking down awareness barriers in our sustainable execution model, and although our data show these barriers have the biggest impact on the cost of execution, we find today's leaders give this leadership trait the least thought. Paying attention to your own personal biases as well as those inherent across the organization are essential to recognizing and resolving barriers to employee engagement and the perceived objectivity of decisions. Accessible leaders are very good at recognizing how their own experience can enable their ability to encourage people, cultures, and organizational silos to work together. Leaders with this trait are not insulated by their fundamental beliefs and preoccupation with activity inside of their own organization, as they have an innate ability to pull their head up and take a look at what's going on around them. Finally, accessible leaders heighten awareness with all stakeholders in their internal and external environments, not just those with whom they enjoy working, and recognize the biases that preference can create. They thrive not only within their own business unit or silo, they reach out to heighten the entire organization's ability to drive results.

We worked with a sales-oriented company that ran into the same execution problem at the end of every quarter – a disproportionate number of orders created an order load that the Sales support team could not handle. Processing orders slowed down at the time speed of business was most critical. The tension between Sales and Support was so ingrained that the organization overlooked the need to resolve the issue. It wasn't until the company hired a new CIO that things began to change. This leader was exceptionally accessible and inspired the organization to enhance their awareness of what was really going on. This leader had the following sub-traits of accessibility.

- **Engage Every Mind.** He immediately brought Sales and Support together to understand what each department could contribute and discuss ways to leverage those contributions to the maximum. Although the CIO found the support team to be more cooperative and easier to work with, he was aware of his bias and conscious of ensuring it did not get in his way. He made sure both teams felt their feedback was "safe in his mouth" and validated so people could understand the situation objectively. For example, one person from the support team complained, "Mike (the VP of Sales) is not the best at developing accurate sales projections." The CIO's response was, "Yes, I'm aware projections are not Mike's strong suit, but he exceeds his sales targets year over year." Validation of a truth or reality is critical, as in this case where it gained the Sales Support team's confidence that the CIO understood that addressing the accuracy of the sales projections was important in resolving the issue. By validating Mike's other contributions, the Support team was also confident the CIO would extend them the same courtesy. By engaging every mind, the CIO was able to reduce distractions from complaints and prior frustrations and move toward a resolution.
- **Build an Accessibility Network.** When people feel they are part of a network, it helps to facilitate a culture of accessibility to make collaboration easier. The CIO knew that taking on this initiative would uncover a number of issues triggered by a myriad of causes. For his team to effectively diagnose problems and identify opportunities, they needed the support of others to accurately pinpoint the source of the failure. As such, the CIO insisted people, including himself, share their personal cell and home phone contact numbers and set the expectation that during high

peak periods, people needed to respond quickly to calls, even if they come in the middle of the night. He was also explicit that "receiving the call" was only half of the equation. Appropriate triage needed to take place to ensure the problem was resolved rapidly and by people closest to the problem. Building an accessibility network means people are both comfortable *seeking* accessibility to what they need and willing to *provide* accessibility to what others need. The CIO participated in as many interactions as possible to build this network. He was active in daily status calls and managed his work and travel schedule to make sure he connected with those in the network as much as possible. Finally, he maintained an open door and tolerated a pragmatic level of drop-in activity in order to foster a culture of accessibility.

- **Seek External Feedback.** Everyone involved in the initiative was aware of the CIO's tendency to schedule periodic feedback meetings over breakfast or coffee to assess the "temperature" of departments involved. Looking and listening outside of his own organization allowed him to "connect the dots" to better align and understand the bigger picture. Strong execution leaders do not rely solely on their own team's word or assumptions – they go to their customers (internal or external) for feedback. The CIO often shared the story of an analyst he worked with for years, but the two had little interaction. Unaware of his contribution, the CIO decided not to fill the analyst's position after retirement. During the three months following the analyst's departure, there was a steady stream of people flowing into the CIO's office looking for information, reports, and data. When he inquired about this increase in activity, he learned that the retired analyst had been an integral source of information to many other people and processes. The moral of his story was to always seek feedback rather than rely on your own perceptions or those that other people formulate for you. It can be eye-opening.

- **Lower Your Defenses.** Finally, accessibility involves two or more parties, so good execution leaders are willing to engage with their defenses down. The CIO had a mantra that every once in a while he'd do a "deep dive" into an issue. Although it took a lot of time to get the full picture, he was willing to incur the delays and additional work. During one of these "deep dives" the CIO became aware that the vice president responsible for support blocked his online calendar every single day from 8 a.m. to 6 p.m. Anyone wanting to meet with him had to email or call his secretary to find a time and provide detail about the meeting request. The secretary would then seek the vice president's approval before releasing a time slot for a meeting. The CIO had never experienced this, as the VP's calendar was open to people at his level and above, just not below. He invited this VP to one of his infamous breakfast meetings and picked the perfect time to ask him to open up his calendar. The CIO explained the importance of keeping the lines of communication open and reiterated how important the VP was to the company's accessibility network.

Prior to the CIO's arrival, the organization was unaware of the problems that plagued the business at the end of each quarter. IT had never supported the Sales team before; however, accessible leadership led the organization to resolve issues quickly, and system performance improvements were made. Within months, the company achieved new record highs for order processing.

The Execution Derailer

Although not unique to a sustainable execution leader, there is one final leadership characteristic that is important to highlight, as it is fatal to sustainable execution. Every organization understands one breach can destroy a culture of trust that took years to establish. We've learned that at the heart of trust are leaders that all have one thing in common – integrity. In sustainable execution, integrity is *the way the leader's actions for driving results are perceived as being honest and of strong ethical principle by others in the organization.* If promotions are perceived to be undeserved or granted because of favoritism, whether true or not, it results in the same outcome. Many senior executives wisely maintain a policy for keeping personal relationships at arm's length for this reason. They realize how it looks when the person who received the promotion is the same person invited to the executive's summer home every year for a weekend of fishing, or the one who stayed after the conference in New York City to do some personal shopping with the boss. Maintaining a "level playing field" does not mean that everyone is given the same opportunity, it means the leader is honest and has strong principles to make sure all are given their deserved opportunity to succeed.

One exceptionally successful CEO who had a reputation for unwavering integrity was masterful at doing "deep dives" to explore information that was at odds with his gut instinct or he found difficult to believe. Some referred to this behavior as a "witch hunt," but the CEO conducted it without bias and blame and took every opportunity to reiterate the intent was to trace and validate information. His story highlights the two primary sub-traits of integrity in sustainable execution.

- **Maintain Objectivity.** Leaders with integrity validate questionable situations and let people know there is a higher court of appeal, as the buck stops with them. More often than not, the CEO found that there was a level of subjectivity or "spin" to information that landed on his desk. He would share his results with his executive team, regardless of how embarrassing it was for those involved. No leader explicitly intends to make people feel self-conscious, but he felt he needed to follow through in this way when execution was not what it should be or if he sensed a high level of unproductive "chirping" (complaining or commenting).

- **Zero Tolerance.** When leaders have integrity, people will tell you that they can "feel" something special in their interactions with them. Strong execution leaders will do their best to protect their part of the organization from the inconsistencies and ploys or tactics that may interfere with their ability to deliver results. Leaders with integrity have broad shoulders, validate situations for themselves, and are willing to engage in difficult conversations to exercise their zero tolerance for gamesmanship and political motivation. They keep people honest in their pursuit of driving results.

If you are a leader who watches people continuously avoid your open door as you ponder why your great strategies and investments are not yielding results, you may wish to try a friendly "deep dive" on a selected issue or two. "Connecting the dots" in this manner usually brings worthwhile insights.

Personal Cost of Execution

When we consider the differentiating attributes of a sustainable execution leader, we begin to understand why people might find it easier to execute in their personal lives than in the corporate environment. These attributes are intrinsically personal and easier to control "at home" than in our corporate practice. Leaders who learn to weave their personal approach to execution into the fabric of the workplace lower their personal cost of execution. This does not suggest they hold work relationships at par with family, it simply suggests they operate with the same principles in both environments, when it comes to fortitude, being resolute, and choosing to be accessible. We close out this chapter with two simple questions you can ask to reflect on your personal cost of execution.

- Can you get the job done? Do you deliver on your commitments, all the time, every time? No excuses.
- If so, at what cost? At a higher cost than your peer? Do you execute seamlessly like a canoe quietly gliding through the water, or is working with you more like a high speed boat that leaves a turbulent wake of destruction and leaves damage in your path?

To achieve sustainable execution, not only do you have to get the job done, you have to consider the cost you incur along the way. Leaders able to keep their personal cost of execution in check will be granted more opportunity to lead future initiatives.

CONCLUSION

We have now covered all of the frameworks, concepts, and approaches that describe a new mindset for sustainable execution. By reducing drag in your execution system, your organization will reap the benefits of flexibility and stability at the same time, which is essential for survival in today's turbulent environment. We conclude the book with a final caution: even in good times, continue to explore potential execution barriers on the horizon. Basking in the glory of your own success has a dark side that few execution experts talk about. Inherent in the concept of sustainable execution is the continuous regime of identifying execution barriers early, and orchestrating the balancing act can help companies remove potential obstacles and sustain performance over the long term. Leveraging structure will gain efficiencies in what is working today, enabling rhythm will ensure responsiveness and agility to tomorrow's new and different influences, and heightening awareness will foster a culture for execution that pays attention to what is really going on and take appropriate action. By following this regime, organizations will look in the mirror to determine how astute they are at managing organizational energy as a scarce and valuable resource and recognize that barriers and threats are at play, even in good times.

To those readers who begin a book by reading the last page, perhaps one of the most profound observations we can share is that our sustainable execution framework applies well beyond the workplace. Though this book was written with the business leader in mind, the frameworks, concepts, and approaches are equally effective in other leadership positions – in family situations, in your Cub Scout troop, in the classroom, in your community of faith, in the basketball team you coach, or in your circle of friends and neighbors. Any situation where people come together to achieve a unified purpose will benefit from shifting toward a new mindset for sustainable execution.

NOTES

Preface

1 Bridges Business Consultancy, "Strategy Implementation Survey Results 2012," https://www.slideshare.net/SpeculandRobin /strategy-implementation-survey-results-2012.
2 R.G. McGrath, "How the Growth Outliers Do It," *Harvard Business Review* 90, no. 1/2 (2012): 110–16.
3 H. Bruch and S. Ghoshal, "Unleashing Organizational Energy," *MIT Sloan Management Review* 45, no. 1 (2003): 45.

Chapter 1

1 Disguised name for a boutique financial services company.
2 A management approach that focuses the organizations on delivering value to the customer, eliminating waste (i.e., activities that don't add value to the end product) and continuous improvement.
3 A collaborative initiative (inspired by hackathons) that brings the organization together for a short collection of activities to inspire intensive collaboration in an effort to create usable sales ideas and approaches.
4 L. Bossidy, R. Charan, and C. Burck, *The Discipline of Getting Things Done* (New South Wales: Random House Business Books, 2002).

5 P. Thean, *Rhythm: How to Achieve Breakthrough Execution and Accelerate Growth* (Austin, TX: Greenleaf Book Group, 2014).

6 P. Thean, *Rhythm: How to Achieve Breakthrough Execution and Accelerate Growth* (City: Leadline, 2016).

7 PwC, "Closing the Gap between Strategy and Execution," 2014, https://www.pwc.com/us/en/advisory/business-strategy-consulting /assets/performance-alignment.pdf.

8 B. Gleeson, "Strategies for Making Organizational Change Stick and Building a Bright Future," *Forbes*, October 31, 2017.

9 Proclinical, *Employee Engagement Report 2017*, 2017, https:// staffscience.proclinical.com/insights/employee-engagement -report-2017.

Chapter 2

1 The methodology used to uncover the twelve execution barriers was root cause analysis (RCA).

2 C. McChesney, S. Covey, and J. Huling, *The 4 Disciplines of Execution: Achieving Your Wildly Important Goals* (New York: Simon and Schuster, 2012).

3 D.N. Sull and C. Spinosa, "Promise-Based Management," *Harvard Business Review* 85, no. 4 (2007): 79–86.

4 A disguised name for a large game and entertainment retail chain.

5 Agile methodology is a type of project management process where solutions evolve through collaboration across self-organizing cross-functional teams and customers.

Part Two

1 Severity is determined by the degree to which participants agree or disagree (6-point scale) to specific items. The score is a percentage of optimal performance. For example, if there are ten indicators related to the Capacity Shift and all are assessed as a 4 on a 6-point scale, the score would be 67 per cent.

Chapter 3

1 J. Maroney, "The Top Three Factors Driving Employee Burnout," *Forbes Magazine*, February 1, 2017.

2 Actionable Intelligence uses decision support and visualization to distribute decision-making amongst a patient's circle of care. Read more in J. Liebowitz and A. Dawson, "Actionable Intelligence in Healthcare," *CRC Press*, April 2017.

3 Advanced triage systems allow the triage nurse to initiate diagnostic protocols for frequently occurring medical problems based on physician-approved algorithms.

4 Telehealth Monitoring Systems provide a way to monitor patients and their needs within the comfort of their own homes.

5 J. Allen and C. Zook, "The Strategic Principles of Repeatability," *Bain & Company Insights*, May 4, 2012.

6 *Survey of America's Physicians: Practice Patterns and Perspectives* (Boston: Physicians Foundation/Merritt Hawkins, 2014).

7 Behold Summit built by IBM and Nvidia performs 20 quadrillion calculations per second. It was described by the *New York Times* as doing 63 billion years of human work in a single second.

8 Crowdsourcing is the practice of obtaining information or input into a task or project by enlisting the services of a large number of people, either paid or unpaid, typically via the internet.

9 S.B. Sitkin, K.E. See, C.C. Miller, M.W. Lawless, and A.M. Carton, "The Paradox of Stretch Goals: Organizations in Pursuit of the Seemingly Impossible," *Academy of Management Review* 36, no. 3 (2011): 544–66.

10 J. Kotter, "Barriers to Change: The Real Reason behind the Kodak Downfall," *Forbes Magazine*, May 2, 2012.

11 J. McNish, "Victim of Success: The Rise and Fall of BlackBerry," Knowledge @ Wharton, December 15, 2015, http://knowledge.wharton.upenn.edu/article/victim-success-rise-fall-blackberry/.

12 S.A. Melnyk, "Lean to a Fault," *CSMP's Supply Chain Quarterly* 3 (2007): 29–33.

13 K. Goetz, "How 3M Gave Everyone Days Off and Created an Innovation Dynamo," fastcodesign.com, February 1, 2011.

14 C. McChesney, S. Covey, and J. Huling, *The 4 Disciplines of Execution: Achieving Your Wildly Important Goals* (New York: Simon and Schuster, 2012).

15 A.M. McGahan, "How Industries Change," *Harvard Business Review* 82, no. 10 (2004): 86–94.

16 The Boston Matrix was developed by the Boston Consulting Group and is an approach to portfolio planning based on relative market share and market growth.

17 Flexible budgets use the revenues and expenses in the current production as a baseline and estimate how the revenues and expenses will change, on the basis of changes in the output. In contrast, static budgets use revenue and expenses in prior years as the baseline, and changes in output are defined as positive or negative variances.

18 R. Horton, P. Searles, and K. Stone. *Integrated Performance Management Plan. Budget. Forecast* (United Kingdom: Deloitte LLP, 201).

19 T. McLaughlin, "Back to Zero: Companies Use 1970s budget Tool to Cut Costs as They Hunt for Growth," Reuters, January 30, 2017, http://www.reuters.com/article/us-usa-companies-budget -idUSKBN15E0CF.

20 J. Heinrich, E. Garton, and B. Martin, "Betting on Zero-Based Budgeting's Trifecta," Bain Insights, October 16, 2016.

21 M.J. Martin, "The Advantages of Using Flexible Budget versus Static Budget," PocketSense, April 19, 2017, http://thefinancebase.com /advantages-using-flexible-budget-vs-static-budget-2813.html.

22 S. Reyburn, "With Acquisition, Sotheby's Shifts Strategy," *New York Times*, January 22, 2016, https://www.nytimes.com/2016/01/25/arts /international/with-acquisition-sothebys-shifts-strategy.html?_r=0.

23 A. Forbes, "Why Sotheby's Just Bought an Art Advisory for $85 Million," *Artsy Editorial*, January 12, 2016.

24 M. Solomon, "Chili's Spends Millions to Make Food Look Good on Social Media, for a Millennial Customer Experience," *Forbes Magazine*, May 24, 2015.

25 Nielsen, "Consumer Trust in Online, Social and Mobile Advertising Grows," *Insights*, April 10, 2012, https://www.nielsen.com/us/en /insights/news/2012/consumer-trust-in-online-social-and-mobile -advertising-grows.html.

26 Accenture analysis; Federal Reserve Board, "Consumers and Mobile Financial Services 2015" (Washington, DC: FRB, March 2015).

27 M. Hirt and P. Willmott, "Strategic Principles for Competing in the Digital Age," *McKinsey Quarterly 5*, no. 1 (May 2014): 1–13.

28 S. Kovac and J. Ruckar, "The Best Online Photo Printing Services of 2019," Reviewed, January 2, 2019, https://www.reviewed.com/home-outdoors/best-right-now/the-best-online-photo-printing-services.

29 A term used to describe an initiative that is given priority but to which no funds are formally allocated.

30 L. Brandes and D. Darai, "The Value and Motivating Mechanism of Transparency in Organizations," *European Economic Review* 98 (2017): 189–98.

Chapter 4

1 J. Straw, B. Davis, M. Scullard, and S. Kukkonen, *The Work of Leaders: How Vision, Alignment, and Execution Will Change the Way You Lead* (San Francisco: John Wiley & Sons, 2013).

2 A visual management approach that provides a graphical representation of work left to do, versus time.

3 L. Bossidy, R. Charan, and C. Burck, *Execution: The Discipline of Getting Things Done*, rev. ed. (New South Wales: Random House, 2002).

4 G. Eckes, *Six Sigma Execution: How the World's Greatest Companies Live and Breathe Six Sigma* (New York: McGraw-Hill, August 2005).

5 D.N. Sull and C. Spinosa, "Promise-Based Management," *Harvard Business Review* 85, no. 4 (2007): 79–86.

6 K.M. Immordino, R.A. Gigliotti, B.D. Ruben, and S. Tromp, "Evaluating the Impact of Strategic Planning in Higher Education," *Educational Planning* 23, no. 1 (2016): 35–48.

7 A performance metric used in strategic management to identify and improve internal functions of a business and their resulting external outcomes. It is used to measure and provide feedback to organizations.

8 Kata is a method of making small, incremental change toward improvements every day.

9 Shmula Contributor, "What Organizations Are Using Kata?" February 4, 2017, http://www.shmula.com/what-organizations-are-using-kata/22057/.

10 C. Espinoza and M. Ukleja, *Managing the Millennials: Discover the Core Competencies for Managing Today's Workforce* (Hoboken, NJ: John Wiley & Sons, 2016).

11 A loosely interpreted meaning of *hoshin* is "setting a direction or setting an objective."

12 Introduced by D. Tapping and T. Shuker, *Value Stream Management for the Lean Office* (Boca Raton, FL: CRC Press, Taylor & Francis Group, 2003).

13 A tool that distributes different forms of accountability by indicating who should be Responsible, Accountable, Consulted, and Informed.

14 A systematic approach of standardizing activities to accomplish a specific organizational goal that makes an organization's workflow more effective, more efficient, and more capable of adapting to an ever-changing environment.

Chapter 5

1 H.K. Gardner, *Smart Collaboration: How Professionals and Their Firms Succeed by Breaking Down Silos* (Boston, MA: Harvard Business Review, 2017).

2 L. Bodell, "5 Ways Process Is Killing Your Productivity," *Fast Company*, May 15, 2012.

3 M. Chui, J. Manyika, J. Bughin, R. Dobbs, C. Roxburgh, H. Sarrazin, G. Sands, and M. Westergren, "The Social Economy: Unlocking the Value and Productivity through Social Technologies," McKinsey Global Institute, July 2012, https://www.mckinsey.com/industries/high-tech/our-insights/the-social-economy.

4 The workathon approach applies Eliyahu Goldratt's theory of constraints to execution as it attempts to reduce the constraints on work that are imposed by the broader organization.

5 Social media (crowdsourcing) platform that allows customers to submit their ideas that are considered by the company's corporate innovation line of business.

6 R. Cross, R. Rebele, and A. Grant, "Collaborative Overload," *Harvard Business Review* 94, no. 1 (2016): 74–9.

7 K. Crowley and K. Elster, *Working with You Is Killing Me: Freeing Yourself from Emotional Traps at Work* (New York: Warner, 2006).

8 Cross, Rebele, and Grant, "Collaborative Overload."

9 B. Cross, *SIMPLE: Killing Complexity for a Lean and Agile Organization* (Boca Raton, FL: Productivity Press, 2017).

10 A business management technique where information is communicated by using visual signals instead of written instructions. The design is deliberate in allowing quick recognition of the information being communicated, in order to increase efficiency and clarity.

11 Chui et al., "Social Economy."

12 S. Holtz, "Organizational Silos Don't Need Busting. They Need Ventilating," Holtz Communication + Technology, March 13, 2014, http://holtz.com/blog/business/organizational-silos-dont-need-busting-they-need-ventilating/4303/.

13 L.-A. Appiah, "Slave-Free Chocolate: A Not-So-Guilty Pleasure," CNN, June 7, 2017, https://www.cnn.com/2017/06/02/world/tonys-chocolonely-slavery-free-chocolate/index.html.

14 A not-for-profit cooperative initiative.

15 B. Boyce, "Collective Impact: Aligning Organizational Efforts for Broader Social Change," *Journal of the Academy of Nutrition and Dietetics* 113, no. 4 (2013): 497.

Chapter 6

1 F. Bevins and A. De Smet, "Making Time Management the Organization's Priority," McKinsey & Company, January 2013, https://www.mckinsey.com/business-functions/organization/our-insights/making-time-management-the-organizations-priority.

2 C. McChesney, S. Covey, and J. Huling, *The 4 Disciplines of Execution: Achieving Your Wildly Important Goals* (New York: Simon and Schuster, 2012).

3 M. Mankins, C. Brahm, and G. Caimi, "Your Scarcest Resource," *Harvard Business Review* 92, no. 5 (2014): 74–80.

4 A North American banking emergency that occurred between 2007 and 2010 and contributed to the economic recession.

5 Name of company is disguised to protect the bank's identity.

6 A term in linear regression used to describe the best-fitting straight line through points of interest – often called the regression line.

7 $100,000 / 50 weeks a year / 40 hours a week = $50.00 an hour x 6 people = $300.

8 J. Gothelf and J. Seiden, *Sense and Respond: How Successful Organizations Listen to Customers and Create New Products Continuously* (Boston: Harvard Business Review, 2017).

9 "2017 Edelman Trust Barometer for the Government of Canada," April 10, 2018.

10 "2018 Sarbanes-Oxley Survey: Benchmarking SOX Costs, Hours and Controls," Protiviti Insights, https://www.protiviti.com/sites /default/files/united_states/insights/sarbanes-oxley_survey_2018 _protiviti.pdf.

11 A. Adkins, "Only One in 10 People Possess the Talent to Manage," *Gallup Workplace*, April 13, 2015.

12 Adecco, "Watch the Skills Gap," January 9, 2019, https://www .adeccousa.com/employers/resources/skills-gap-in-the-american -workforce/.

13 PayScale is a research and talent management company dedicated to helping address the skills gap by identifying skills that are most important and valued by today's organizations.

14 C. Bhuiya, "The Skills Gap Is Real: 8 Skills You Didn't Know You Needed," Go Skills, https://www.goskills.com/Soft-Skills/Articles /Skills-gap.

15 Seinfeld, "Reservations," YouTube, November 15, 2007, https://www .youtube.com/watch?v=A7uvttu8ct0.

16 C. Jenkin, "Emails Expected to Rise to 140 a Day in 2018," News.com .au, http://www.news.com.au/finance/work/emails-expected-to -rise-to-140-a-day-in-2018/news-story/c51f74f31e3fe6af2472f723e65ce493.

17 Daily Management is the system that delivers customer value through proper support and leadership to those who are closest to the process (customers and process owners) – elements commonly used include daily routine, visual control boards, and daily accountability.

INDEX

Figures and tables indicated by page numbers in italics.